PHILOTHEUS OR THEOPHILOS

Theodoret

Bishop of Cyrrhus

Translated by: D.P. Curtin

Copyright @ 2021 Dalcassian Press

All rights reserved. No part of this publication may be reproduced, distributed, or transmitted in any form or by any means, including photocopying, recording, or other electronic or mechanical methods, without the prior written permission of the publisher, except in the case of brief quotations embodied in critical reviews and certain other non-commercial uses permitted by copyright law. For permission request, write to Dalcassian Press at dalcassianpublishing at gmail.com

ISBN: 979-8-3302-3475-2 (Paperback)

Library of Congress Control Number:
Author: Curtin, D.P. (1985-)

Printed by Ingram Content Group, 1 Ingram Blvd, La Vergne, Tennessee

First printing edition 2021.

PHILOTHEUS OR THEOPHILOS

CHAPTER I: JAMES OF NISIBIS

Moses, that divine lawgiver, who opened the bottom of the sea, and covered the dry desert with the inundation of waters, and did all other miracles, wrote down the deeds of those saints who were of old: not the practical wisdom which he had received from the Egyptians, but the splendor of grace received from above. For from where else would Abel have learned virtue, and Enoch the study of virtue, and Noah justice, and Melchizedek the pious priesthood, Abraham's calling, faith, fortitude, and hospitality, which was of great concern to him, the popular sacrifice of his son, and a catalog of other things that he had done in a remarkable manner And to sum up, the struggles, the victories, the proclamations of the divine men, unless he had received the rays of an intelligent and divine Spirit? This, too, I need help at the present time, for I am trying to write the lives of the saints who rose to fame a little before us and in our times, and I would like to set forth, as it were, certain laws for those who wish to imitate them. Therefore, the prayers of these are to be invoked, and we must begin to tell.

Nisibis is a city on the border between the kingdoms of the Romans and the Persians. The great James arose from it, embraced a solitary and quiet life, and occupied the summits of the highest mountains, and spent his life in them. In spring, indeed, both in summer and autumn, he used the woods, and had the sky as a roof; but in the wintertime, he welcomed the cave itself, which afforded him a little shelter. And he had food, not that which is born and sown with labor, but that which is produced of its own accord: already gathering from the wild trees the fruits which grow spontaneously, and from the herbs those which are edible, and are considered like vegetables, from these he gave the body what was sufficient for to live, refusing the use of fire. The use of wool was also superfluous for him; for the roughest goats of the village filled its use, and from them it was made both a coat and a simple clothe. Thus afflicting the body, he constantly offered spiritual nourishment to the body, and purifying the contemplation of the faculty of thought, and making the mirror transparent to the divine Spirit, with his revealed face, by the divine apostle's sentence, beholding the glory of the Lord, he was transformed into the same image from glory to glory, as if by the spirit of the Lord (1 Cor. 3). Hence the trust in God that was of God increased day by day, and when he asked God for what he needed to ask, he immediately received it. Furthermore, from here too he foresaw the future prophetically, and received the power to perform miracles from the grace of the most holy Spirit. I will relate a few of these and open the ray of his apostolic splendor to those who do not know. At that time madness prevailed in the idols of men, and indeed inanimate statues claimed divine worship for themselves, but the worship of God was neglected by the majority, and they adored the workman of all things.

At that time, he had come to Persia, he was going to see the plants of true religion, and he was going to take care of them as much as he could. And when he had passed the spring, certain girls, who were washing clothes, and cleaning their clothes with their feet, not even new, and who carried a decent weight before them, were in a respectful manner; but, stripped of their shame, and with their faces rubbed, and with impudent eyes, they looked at the divine man, neither covering their heads, nor taking down the clothes they had put on. When the man of God bore this with pain and wished to show the power of God in time, that by a miracle he might deliver him from impiety, he indeed cursed the fountain, and the flow immediately disappeared. He cursed the girls also and chastised their impudent youth by bringing in a dog before the time, and a conversation ensued, and their hair was changed to black, and they became like newly planted trees, which are in spring covered with autumn leaves. And when they had thus felt the execution (for they had fled by the flowing spring, and looking at each other's heads, they saw that sudden change), they hurried to the city, to report what had happened. But when they ran, and encountered the great James, they besought him to control his anger, and to remit the execution. But he did not hesitate long. Indeed, he offered prayers to the Lord, but he ordered them to flow again. She, however, soon again emanated from her penetratives, just diverted by nods. And when they had obtained this, they asked that the hair of their daughters also be restored to its own color. And they say that he also granted this, but demanded the girls who had received that discipline, and since they did not come, he left the execution, a document of restraint, and an argument of restraint, and a permanent and evident reminder of divine power. Such is the miracle of this new Moses, which indeed was not done by the stroke of a rod but took effect by the sign of the cross. Now, besides the miracle, I also greatly marvel at the meekness; for he did not, like the great Elisha, deliver those impudent girls to the wild bears; but by a kind of innocuous discipline, and which had little indecency, he taught at the same time piety and self-control. But I said these things, not to accuse the prophet of cruelty (far from being so insane), but to show that when he had the same power, he did those things which were in accordance with the greatness of Christ and the New Testament.

When he once saw that a Persian judge had given an unjust sentence, he cursed a certain great stone, which was near the site, and ordered it to be broken up and scattered, and to accuse him of his unjust sentence. And the stone was immediately broken into innumerable pieces, and those who were present were crushed; but the judge, filled with horror, indeed recalled the former, but gave the second just sentence. And here too he imitated his Lord, who, when he wanted to show that he willingly and willingly suffered suffering, and easily if he had wanted to punish the criminals, he did not inflict punishment on them, but by drying up the dead fig with his word, he showed his prowess (Matt. 21). He also, imitating this clemency, did not punish the unjust judge, but taught him justice with the blow of a stone.

When he was remarkable for these things, loved by all, and was on the lips of all, he was drawn to the office of priest, and presided over his country. But when he had changed that mountain way of life and had not taken up the civil habit of life by decision of his own mind, he neither changed his food, nor his clothing; but the places were indeed changed, but the organization of life received no change. Indeed, the labors were increasing, and were far greater than before. For the fasting, and the bed on the ground, and the sack in which he was clothed, had also completely attended to the care of those who were in need; that, I say, he was concerned about widows, and provided for orphans, and rebuked those who did wrong, and brought just help to those who were wronged. And what is the need to review everything with those who know what is appropriate for those who receive this treatment? But in a remarkable way he embraced such labors, as one who would remarkably both desire and fear the master of the sheep.

And the greater the riches of virtue he gathered, the greater the grace of the most holy Spirit did he enjoy; and when he was sometimes on his way to a certain village or town (for I do not have enough room), some poor people approached him, presenting one of them who was with them as if he were dead, and demanding from him the things necessary to bury him. And he indeed yielded to those who asked, and offered prayers to God as if for a dead man, begging him to forgive him what he had sinned in life, and to condescend to admit him into the dance of the righteous. And when these things were said, the soul of him who then feigned death flew away, and coverings were provided for his body. But after the admirable man had advanced a little, those who had composed the act ordered him who was lying down to rise. And when they saw that he would not hear him, and that it was pretended that the truth had escaped, and that the person had changed into his true face, they went to the great James, and imploring him imploringly, and fell at his feet, and had undertaken an act which they had done recklessly, saying that the cause was poverty. They begged him to send them his crime, and to restore the soul which had been taken to him who was lying. Therefore, imitating the Lord's clemency, he also heard the prayers, and showed a miracle, that he who had been taken away by prayers restored life to a lying person through prayers. But this indeed seems to me to be similar to the great miracle of Peter, who delivered Ananias and Sapphira to death when they had been robbed and lied to (Acts 5). In fact, in the same way here, he who had stolen the truth and used lies took away his soul. But when he had learned of the theft (for he had revealed it by the grace of the Spirit), he brought about the execution; but this act, not knowing the argument, offered prayers indeed, but stopped the course of life for him who had pretended. And indeed, the divine Apostle did not at all deliver the dead from calamity; for the beginnings of saving preaching had need of fear. Now when he was full of apostolic grace, he punished him for a time, and soon remitted the punishment. For this work he had to do to gain those who had offended.

But we must go to other things, and they are to be explained briefly. For after Arius, the father and maker of blasphemy and blasphemy against the only-begotten and most holy Spirit, moved against him who had made him himself, filled Egypt with tumult and confusion, and Constantine the greatest emperor, Zerubbabel of our flock (for like him he brought back all the captivity of the pious from exile, and divine he raised up the temples scattered on the ground and raised them up high) after he had assembled all the prefects of the churches of Nicaea at that time, the great James also came with others, to contend for the true decrees, as a valiant man and leader of the whole phalanx. For the empire of the Romans was then comparable to Nisibis. But after that sacred assembly had been dismissed, and every man had returned to his own place, he also returned here as a mighty man victorious, rejoicing over the trophies of piety.

But when some time had passed, that great and admirable emperor indeed departed from life with the crown of piety; and his sons were to be the heirs of the kingdom of the world. Then the king of the Persians, whose name was Sapores, despising his sons, because their power was not equal to their father's, made war against Nisibis with a great force of both horse and foot. He also led a great number of elephants, and divided the army to besiege the city. . Then, placing the archers there, and ordering them to shoot weapons at those who were on the walls, he ordered others to dig below and pull down the walls. But after all things were void and void to him, that the things of the divine man might be dissolved by the prayers; and lastly, when the river was passing by, relying on a great number of men, he had stopped the flow, and having built walls, and having gathered together a great quantity of the river with obstructions to hold it back, he threw it all at once into the walls, using it as some most powerful machine. But they did not bear the blow of the water but were shaken by the onslaught and fell completely on that side. They, however, raised a great clamor, as if the city was already an easy capture; for the inhabitants of the city were ignorant of the great wall: yet they put off breaking it, when they saw that the city could not be approached on account of the waters. When, therefore, they had retired a great distance, as if their labor were about to cease, they rested themselves, and took care of their horses; but those who inhabited the city were heartily converted to supplications, having the great James as their intercessor. And those who were still alive in age, all rebuilt with the greatest effort they could, not taking any care of beauty or orderly framework, but all components at random, both stones and bricks, and whatever each one carried. so that it would be sufficient to prevent the running of horses, and the ascent of men without stairs. Then all ask the executioners of the man of God, that he may show himself on the walls, and throw weapons of curses at the enemies. He, however, being exhorted, went up, and beholding many thousands of them, besought God to send down upon them a cloud of flies and gnats. And indeed he said, God sent, having been urged by him as by Moses, and the men indeed were wounded by the divine weapons, while the horses and elephants fled with their chains broken, scattered hither and thither, so that those who could not bear the thorns When, therefore, the impious king saw that the machines were of no use to him, and that the intrusion of the water was useless (for the wall that had fallen had been rebuilt), and that the whole army was afflicted with labors, and that he was ill under the god, and was afflicted by the divinely sent plague: he saw but the divine man also walking on the walls, and having conjectured that the emperor himself was in charge of the work (for he had appeared to him and was clothed in purple, and redeemed with a diadem), was indeed indignant at those who had deceived him, and had persuaded him to stir up war, and had said that the emperor was not present. and when he had condemned them by the head, he dismissed the army, and returned as quickly as possible to his kingdom. In this also Hezekiah God performed miracles, not less than them, but even greater, as it seems to me. For when the wall fell, the city was not taken, what greater miracle could there be? Besides this, I also greatly admire that, when he used curses, he did not ask that lightning and thunderbolts be sent down from heaven, as did the great Elijah, when each man of fifty came to him with his fifty. For he had heard that the Lord had said plainly to James and John, who were trying to do this very thing: You do not know whose spirit you are after (Luke 9). And therefore, he did not ask that the land should give way to them, nor did he ask that the phalanx should be consumed by fire; but that they should be sacrificed to those little animals; and when he had come to know the power of God, at last he had changed and learned piety and the true worship of God. This divine man had so much confidence in God, he obtained so much grace from above. When he was constantly engaged in these things, and daily increased in divine things, when he laid down this life with the greatest glory and departed from these places. And when some time had passed, and this city, which was then in command, had been handed over to the kingdom of the Persians, all those who lived in it went out, carrying the body of their defender and prince, indeed bearing it painfully and grieving that they had to cross over, singing and celebrating the valor of the mighty the winner For if he had lived, they would never have come under the power of the barbarians. When I have reviewed these things about the divine man, I will pass on to another narrative, asking that I may obtain his blessing.

CHAPTER II: JULIAN SABAS

Julianus, whom the inhabitants called by the surname of honoring Saba, and πρεσβύτην, that is, old man, the Greek word signifies this name, in a region which was once of the Parthians, but is now called the Osroenes, fixed a hut for monastic training. And it extends to the West, indeed, as far as the bank of the river, and its name is Euphrates; but to the East, the sun, has the limit of the Roman empire. For Assyria welcomes the Persians, since the western end of the kingdom of the Persians is the western end, which those who followed afterwards named Adiabene. In this nation there are indeed many large and populous cities; and much of the region is indeed inhabited, but much of it is both uninhabitable and deserted. When this divine man had arrived at the extremity of this solitude, and had found a cave not made by hands, nor well and neatly dug, but that it might afford some little shelter to those who took refuge in it, he willingly settled in a place glittering with gold and silver, thinking it to be royal more magnificent And he dwelt there, taking food once a week: and the food was barley bread, and then bran; and the obsonium, salt; and a very sweet drink, in itself native to flowing water; and this was not measured by satiety, but was first defined for himself by the use of the lower. But they were the delights of the people and the most delicious food, the singing of Davidic hymns, and constant conversation with God. And when he enjoyed them insatiably, he never wanted to be satisfied with them; but indeed, it was always filled, and always cried out: How sweet are your words to my throat! on the honey and the honeycomb in my mouth (Ps. 118) For again he heard the blessed David saying: The true judgments of the Lord, justified in the same, are more desirable than gold and precious stones, and sweeter than honey and honeycomb (Ps. 18). Again, he heard him say: Delight in the Lord, and he will give you the requests of your heart (Ps. 36). And again, Let the heart of those who seek the Lord rejoice (Ps. 14). And: Make my heart rejoice, that it may fear your name. And: Taste and see how kind the Lord is (Ps. 33). And: My soul thirsts for the mighty living God (Ps. 41). And: My soul clings to you. And he who said these things transferred his love to himself. For this reason, the great David also taught these things by singing, that he might establish many associates and rivals in loving God. Nor indeed is hope false; but he saved both this divine man and innumerable others with divine love. For he was so enflamed with the fire of love that he became intoxicated with longing and saw nothing of earthly things; but he dreamed only of his beloved at night and caught him by vision during the day. Many people had learned this sum of his philosophy, some who lived nearer, and others who lived further away. For the report spread in all directions, and supplicants ran to be partakers of the wrestling, and to live to posterity to him as the master of the exercise and the parents of the children. For birds are not only hunted by singing, and calling them to themselves, which are of the same kind, and entangling the subjects in snares; but men also hunt those who are of the same nature, some to destruction, others to salvation. Thus, gathered together there were soon ten, and then twice and three times as many. But when there were so many of them, he received that cave; for they had learned from the old man to neglect the care of the body. But after a certain time and gathering the herbs that grew of their own accord, then filling the vessels, and mixing as much of the muriale as was sufficient, they had that food which they needed for treatment. But to these vegetables moist habitations are most injurious; for by their very nature, they are wont to breed decay and rot. At first he did not at all admit to the demand; but at last he was persuaded (for he had learned from the great Paul not to seek what is his own (1 Cor. 13), but to concede something and to accommodate himself to the lowly), indeed he gave the little house a certain short and small measure, and went far away from the cave, he was going to offer the usual supplications to God. For he was wont to go often fifty stadia, and sometimes even twice as many into the desert, and separating himself from all human habit, and returning to himself, to meet and converse with God by himself, and to contemplate that divine and ineffable beauty. When they had taken this leisure, which they thought worthy to be carried out by him, they built a little house, corresponding to the use, indeed, in just symmetry, but larger than they had ordered. And on the tenth day, as Moses indeed returned from the mountain, and from that which cannot be explained in words by contemplation, when he had seen the building made greater than he wanted, I fear, O men, lest while we enlarge the earthly dwellings, we should diminish the heavenly ones: but these things are indeed for a time , and what suits us for a moment, but heavenly things are eternal, and which can take no end. And these things indeed he said, teaching the choir those things which are more perfect;

PHILOTHEUS OR THEOPHILOS

He endured, however, when he heard the apostolic voice: I seek not what is good for me, but what is good for many, that they may be kept (1 Cor. 10). He also taught them, indeed, to offer a common hymnody to God within, but after dawn the two to go out together into the wilderness: and one, bending his knees, to offer the adoration, which is due to the Lord, while the other, standing, sings the fifteen psalms of David. Then they changed their work, one rising to sing, and the other prostrating on the ground to worship, and this they did constantly from morning until dusk. But before the setting of the sun, resting a little in the cave, these indeed from this side, and those from that side, indeed all of them from every direction gathered into the cave, and offered the evening hymns together to the Lord. And the old man himself was wont to take one of the most distinguished as his partner in office.

And he was followed most frequently by a certain man of the Persian race, whose body was large and admirable, but whose body possessed a more admirable soul. And his name was James, who, even after his death, shone forth in all his power. He was distinguished and illustrious, not only among those who were there, but also among those who were in the schools of philosophy or monasteries in Syria, in which he also ended his life, having lived, as is said, one hundred and four years. When he was a great old man on the road to the wilderness, he followed him at a distance. For the teacher would not allow him to approach nearer, lest the opportunity of disputing should be taken away from him; but the word would distract the mind from the contemplation of God. And as he followed, he saw a great dragon on the road; then, having looked upon him, he did not indeed dare to advance; but when he had often wished to turn away from him for fear, he strengthened his mind again. Then when he stooped down and took the stone and threw it, he saw that the dragon remained in the same position, unable to move at all. But when he understood that he was dead, he thought that the old man's death must have been the death of the beast. And when the journey was finished, and the service of hymns completed, when the time for rest had come, and the old man was sitting down, he also ordered him to give his body to rest for a little while, for at first, he sat in silence. And when he had allowed him to ask, he said, "I saw a great dragon lying in the road, and at first, I was afraid, supposing him to be alive; Tell me, said he, O father, who slew him? For you went before, but no one else passed this way. And the old man: Cease, says he, to inquire curiously about them, which cannot bring any benefit to those who are ignorant. However, the wonderful James insisted on nothing else, desiring to know the truth. And the old man, indeed, for a long time trying to conceal it, but not bringing his friend to anger any longer: I, said he, will tell you, if you desire to know it; and they often excite pride; but if I should depart hence, and be freed from such perturbations of mind, I do not forbid you to speak and narrate the power of divine grace. Know then, says the great Julian, that the beast attacked me as I was coming, and opened her mouth, desiring to dev rare; but I, calling Jesus, and pointing with my finger to the trophy of the cross, shook off all fear; and praising the common Savior, I went on. Having thus finished the narrative, he went to the cave.

Once upon a time a young man, born in a noble place, but gently brought up, and showing greater readiness and vigor of mind than his strength could bear, asked the old man to accompany him on the journey into the wilderness, not indeed that which they all took every day, but a very long one, and in which it was often eight or ten days to travel. And this was the most famous Asterius. But when the divine old man stopped the young man and said that it was a dry and destitute of water, the young man insisted, begging him to grant him this gift. But the old man, overcome by prayers, gave way; but he followed, at first eagerly. But when the first, second, and third days had passed, and he was scorched by the rays of the sun (for it was summer, and in the height of summer the flame of the sun is certainly more burning), he labored continually with thirst. And for the first time he was ashamed to reveal his illness, remembering what had been said to him by his teacher. But at last, he was defeated, and quite utterly failing, he begged the old man to have mercy on him. But when he had recalled to his memory what he had foretold, he ordered him to return. But when the youth said that he did not know the way that leads to the cave, nor if he did know, could he go, since his strength was spent with thirst; The divine man, pitying the youth's accident, and forgiving the infirmity of his body, bent his knees and prayed to the Lord, and with warm tears he watered the soil and asked for the way of salvation for the youth. But he who does the will of those who fear him, and hears their prayer, caused the drops of tears that touched the dust to be a fountain of waters, and thus filled with the flow, he ordered the youth to depart immediately. And the fountain remained to this day, bearing witness to the divine prayer of the old man. For how once he, when he struck that barren rock with his rod, caused it to produce overflowing river waters, to satisfy those many thousands of people exhausted by thirst; thus, when he had watered that very dry sand with tears, he caused fountains to emanate flowing; not as a multitude of multitudes, but as a remedy for the thirst of one young man. For his soul, enlightened by divine grace, clearly foresaw the future perfection of the young man. For many times later he was challenged by divine grace, that he might exercise many others to the same grace, in the places which are about Gendarum (which is the largest village under Antioch) he established a monastic gymnasium, and indeed he drew many other athletes of philosophy to him.

And he also drew the great Acacius, distinguished, I say, and of great renown, who was indeed excellent in monastic life, and sent forth splendid rays of virtue, so that he who was worthy of habit should become priest, and Berhoea was assigned to feed. But when he had been entrusted with the care of the flock for fifty-eight years, he did not indeed leave the form of monastic life, but at the same time moderated both monastic and civil virtue; and indeed, taking the exact perfection of that, and the economy and dispensation of the latter, he forced into one those things which were separated from one another.

But Asterius was the hunter and exerciser of this virtue, who was always held in such great love by that great old man, that he often went to him twice a year, often even thrice. When he came, he used to bring carts to the members, loading three or four cattle. But gathering two of them, so that they would suffice the old man for the whole year, he laid the burden on his shoulders, calling himself the master's beast and offering it. And he carried that burden, making a journey of seven days, not ten or twenty stadia. But when an old man had once seen him carrying a load of burdens on his shoulder, carrying it with difficulty, he said that these should not be presented to him as food; for it would not be just that he should indeed undergo so much labor, while he himself should delicately enjoy the sweat of it. And when he had sworn that he would not lay the burden from his shoulders, unless the old man agreed, he would partake of the food that had been brought: For in this also he imitated the first of the apostles, who, when the Lord wished to wash his feet, first denied it, clearly affirming that it would not happen (John 13). But when he heard that he would be cut off from the Lord's communion unless he granted this, he prayed that he might wash his hands and head in addition to his feet. Even so the excellent John was ordered to wash the Savior, indeed before he confessed his servitude, and showed the Lord. And afterwards he carried out the commandment, not behaving harshly, but yielding to the Lord. In this way also this divine man was indeed burdened by laboring for another to enjoy food himself; but when he saw the ardent zeal of his client's mind, he preferred his service to his will.

PHILOTHEUS OR THEOPHILOS

Perhaps some one of those who derive great pleasure from the criticism of others and have only learned to laugh at things that are honorable, will say that this narrative is not worthy to be remembered. And I have added this also to the other miracles of this man, not only wishing to show the piety of great men towards him, but also to declare the gentleness and moderation of his manners, thinking that he was agreeable. For when he was so great and of such virtue, he did not consider himself worthy of even the slightest honor but rejected him as one who in no way belonged to him. And again, he supported him, that he might affect those who did them with favor.

But fleeing (for he who had escaped to all was evident, drawing to himself by the fame of those who are good and honorable lovers) he came to Mount Sinai with a few of his little relatives: not entering a town, not a village, but entering a road through an impassable wilderness. He also carried on his shoulders the necessary food, bread and salt, a flagon and a wooden cup, and a sponge tied with a rope; so that if they ever found deeper water, they would indeed drain the sponges, but drink it pressed into a cup. When, therefore, they had completed a journey of many days, they arrived at the desired mountain; and when they had worshiped their Lord, they spent a long time there continually, considering the solitude of the place and the rest of the soul to be the greatest pleasure. And when, in that rock under which Moses, the leader of the prophets, was hiding, a habit worthy of one who saw God as he could be seen, he had built a church and consecrated the divine altar, which also remained to this day, he returned to his palace.

And when he, who indeed had the same name as himself, but understood the threats of the impious emperor (for the pious, threatened with utter destruction, had set out for the Persians, and who felt the same as he did, eagerly awaited his abominable return), then he prayed to God with great earnestness and offering it with a strong desire, and extending it to the tenth day, he heard a voice saying, that cursed and stinking swine had been removed from the midst. But not having received the end of the prayer, he immediately ended the prayer, but changed the petition into the singing of a hymn, giving thanks to his Savior, and his mercy and the power of the enemy of foreigners. For a very long time he was gracious and gentle to the wicked; but when his gentleness and patience had driven the criminal to a greater rage, he opportunely brought about the execution. But when he had finished his prayer, and had turned to his own people, it was clear that he was in a happy and tranquil mood; for the cheerfulness of his mind showed a cheerful countenance. But when those who were engaged with him were amazed at the new spectacle (for when he was always seen with a sad aspect, then he was seen to smile), and when they asked for a reason for joy, he said, O brothers, the present time is for joy; for the wicked ceased, as is the voice of Isaiah (Is. 24), and gave the merits of bold undertakings punishments; and he who exercised tyranny against God, who made and preserved him, was rightly slain by the right hand of him who was equal to his rule. Therefore, I am glad when I see the churches that have been attacked by him rejoicing, and I see that the villain obtained no help from those whom he worshiped as demons. He therefore had such a foreknowledge of the murder of this wicked man.

But when Valens, who after him took the reins of the Roman empire, abandoned the truth of the evangelical dogmas, and accepted the imposture of the error of Arius, then a greater storm arose against the Church. when the captains were indeed expelled from every side, but certain robbers and enemies were sufficient to take their place. But I will not recount the whole tragedy at present, I will pass over others for now, but I will only mention one, which clearly shows the grace of the divine Spirit flourishing in this old man. Indeed, the great Meletius had been expelled from the church of Antioch, which had been entrusted to him by God as the shepherd of the universe. And now, indeed, coming into some cave of the mountain, they celebrated the sacred assembly there; but now they made the bank of the river an oratory, and sometimes a military gymnasium, which was situated before the northern gate. For they did not allow those who waged war to remain in one place. Now the students were hurling lies; and they had spread a rumor in that city, that a great man, here I say an old man, had embraced the communion of the dogmas of religion which they themselves held. This greatly distressed the pious, lest the report, deceiving the ruder and simpler, should entangle them in the snares of the heretics.

But the godly and blessed men, Flavianus and Diodorus, who were considered worthy to be the sacrificers, and to preside over the pious people, and Aphraates, whose life, if God has granted you, I will add, persuade that great Acacius, of whom we have mentioned, to accept the count of the road his master, and the disciple of the holy old man, that distinguished Asterius, would run to the common splendor of piety, and the support of evangelical doctrine, and would persuade him to abandon that way of going about in solitude, and come to bring help to so many thousands who were perishing by fraud, and by his dew Aryan's arrival would extinguish the flame. The divine Acacius ran, and taking, as he had been commanded, the great Asterius, came to the greatest light of the church; and when he had greeted him, he said, "Tell me, O father, for what reason do you endure all this labor so willingly?" And when he had answered: The worship of God is more precious to me, both in body, and soul, and life, and in all things that pertain to life; but I try, as far as I can do for him, to offer him a service free from dirt, and to please him constantly; I will show you, says Acacius, the means by which you will serve him more than now; and I will say this, not using reasoning alone, but as one who has learned from his teaching. For when he once asked Peter whether he loved him more than others, and learned what he knew even before Peter's voice, for you, he says, know, Lord, that I love you (John 21); He showed him what the agent should worship him more. For if you love me, he says, feed my sheep and feed my lambs. This too, O Father, must be done for you; for there is a danger lest the sheep perish by the wolves; but he loves them very much, who is very much loved by you. But it is proper for lovers to do those things which, when done, are pleasing to those who are loved. And otherwise, there is no small danger, the loss of many and great of those sweats, if you could suffer them to neglect, to pass by in silence, indeed, that the truth would be seriously attacked, and those who adhere to it would be captured; but to those who are to be hunted, the appeal of your name is meat. For the governors of Arius boast of having you as a partner in their impiety and boast of their abomination. When the old man heard this for the first time, ordering quiet to prevail for a time, and not the noise of the city, as he was not accustomed to them, he fled and ran to Antioch. And when he had completed a journey of two or three days in the wilderness, he came at night to a certain farm: and when a certain rich woman heard that sacred dance coming, she ran to receive their blessing; and, falling at their feet, begged that his house might be their inn. The old man agreed, and that since he had been separated from such a spectacle for more than forty years. And when that wonderful woman was occupied in ministering to those holy men, a child seven years old, whose mother was alone, who had rivaled the hospitality of Sarah, and it was evening and dark, fell into the well. But when, as is reasonable, a tumult had arisen from it, and the mother perceived it, she indeed commanded all to be quiet; and putting the lid on the well, he insisted on the service. And when the table was set before the divine men, the divine old man commanded that the child of the woman should be called and receive a blessing. But when the wonderful woman said that he was ill, she continued to order him to be taken away. And after the woman had told him what had happened, the old man left the table, and running to the well, when he had ordered the cover to be removed, and a light to be brought, he saw a boy sitting on the surface of the water, and beating the water with his hand in a childish manner, and who had been thought to be destroyed, thinking it a game ; and when they had tied some ropes and let them down, they pulled out the boy; and the boy immediately ran to the old man's feet, saying that he had seen him carrying himself in the water, and preventing him from drowning. The woman received this reward of hospitality from the blessed old man.

And to pass over other things that happened on the journey, they indeed came to Antioch; and all came together from every quarter, desiring to see the man of God, and each desiring to receive medicine for his disease: but he dwelt in the caves which were on the side of the mountain; where they also say that the divine apostle Paul lived and hid. But as soon as they all knew that he was a man, he was seized with a most violent fever. And when the great Acacius saw the great multitude of those who were gathered together, and what had happened, he bore the sickness with great pain (for he estimated that those who had assembled would be troubled if the men should recover the disease, from whose hand they hoped to find a cure): Do not be troubled in heart, said the old man. ; for if health is necessary, the Lord will give it at once. Immediately, therefore, after these words he turned to prayer, and as was his wont, bending his knees and forehead to the ground, begged that he might be healed, if there should be any benefit from it to those who had come together. He had not yet finished his prayers, and suddenly a great flow of sweat extinguished the flame of fever.

And when he had delivered many from diseases of every kind, he went to a meeting of the pious. And when he was passing through the royal gates, a certain beggar who used his legs for feet and was being dragged along the ground, when he stretched out his hand and touched his cloak, he indeed drove out the disease by faith, but running out he showed that he was running as well as before the disease, doing the same thing as the lame man whom Peter and they raised John (Acts 3). When this was done, all the people of the city flocked together: and there was a warlike gymnasium full of those who concurred. But the slanderers and liars were affected by shame, but the students of the truth were happy and calm in spirit. From here they drew the light of truth into their homes, those who needed to be cared for. And a certain man to whom the greatest command of the magistrates, and to whom the nail of the East was committed, sent to him, begging him to come to him, and deliver him from an urgent disease. He, however, came without any hesitation, and with a common prayer to the Lord he relieved his illness with a word, and ordered him to give thanks to God.

When he had done these and such things, he decided to return to the hut of his monastic practice. And when he was on his way through Cyrus (this city is two days' journey from Antioch), he was indeed diverted to the house of the illustrious martyr Dionysius: and those who were there in charge of the worship of God and of the right religion, besought those who were convenient to bring him help to those who were awaiting the foreseeable destruction. For they said that Asterius, who had been brought up in the sophistic and false art of disputing, and had thrown himself into the church of heretics, and had attained the episcopal office, fiercely defended falsity, and used the impious artifice against the truth; and fear us, they said, lest by covering up falsity like a kind of bait, and extending the connections of syllogisms like a kind of net, he should catch many of the simpler ones; for it was for this reason that he was accused by his adversaries. And the old man said: Be of good spirit, and supplicate God with us, adding prayer and physical affliction to prayers. When these prayed to God in this way, one day before the festive and celebrated day, on which the defender of falsehood and the enemy of the truth was about to speak, he received a divinely sent plague, and when he had been ill only one day, he passed away alive, hearing that voice, as is probable: Fool , this night they will take your soul from you (Luke 12) But if you have prepared nets and snares, you will be entangled in them, and not others. These things also happened to Balaam, who himself, having risen up against the people of God, when some impious Balak had conspired against him, gave him punishments, as if he had been slain by the Israelite right hand (Num. 24) . Therefore, even here, when he had devised some clever ideas against the people of God, he was deprived of the life of the people by God. Cyrus obtained this salvation through his prayer.

And these things which I have told, the great Acacius delivered to me the divine head, who knew well all that had been done by him. When, therefore, he had gone thither, and returned to his companions, and had been with them not a little time, he passed over to the life of old age and trouble with great promptness and zeal, as one who had meditated incorruption in mortal nature, but expected the immortality of the body. I, however, stopping here to pray for him, will pass on to another: asking the saints who enter into this narrative, through their intercession, to win for me the benevolence of heaven.

CHAPTER V: PUBLIUS

At the same time there was a certain Publius, who, on account of his form, was worthy of consideration, and endowed with a soul which suited his form, or rather, showing it in a more admirable body. He was indeed descended from the senatorial order, and was born in the city where that Xerxes, whose reputation is so famous everywhere, was making war on Greece, and desiring to cross the river Euphrates with his army. After the bridge was built, he called the place Zeugma, that is, the junction, and named the city from the fact. He arose from her, and was procreated from such a race, occupying a high place, which was not more than thirty stadia distant from the city. There, when he had built a small little house, he sold all that he had received from his father; house, I say, and possessions, and flocks, and clothes, and vessels of silver and brass, and if there was anything else with these. And when, by the divine law, he had divided them among those to whom it was necessary, and had freed himself from all earthly care, he undertook that one care for all, namely, to serve him who had called him; and he was constantly turning it over in his mind, at night and for a long time considering and examining how he might increase it. For this reason, his labor increased every day, became greater and more intense day by day, and was full of sweetness and pleasure, and drove satiety far away. For no one ever saw him resting, even for the smallest part of the day, but psalmody was indeed prayer, and prayer was psalmody, and both were received by the reading of divine discourses. Then the guests who came were taken care of, and then some of the necessary work was done. Entering these paths of life and setting forth a model of virtue to those who wished to be imitated, like a kind of songbird, he forced many of his kind into these saving nets. Moreover, from the beginning, he suffered from having no one to live with him: but building small houses near the doors, he ordered each of those who met to live by himself: often visiting the houses and examining whether they had any storage other than use. And they say that he also, approaching the balance, carefully weighed the measure of bread; and if he ever found more than was determined, he took it hard, and called those who did this hellenous. For he ordered neither those who eat nor drink to wait for satiety; but he took only what was sufficient to preserve the life of the body; and if he ever saw even flour covered with bran, he attacked those who had done this with curses, as those who enjoyed the delicacies of the Sybarites. Moreover, even at night, coming unexpectedly to the door of each one, if he found any one watching and praising God, he retired silently; but if he sensed someone sleeping, he would indeed knock on the door with his hand, but his tongue would be driven into the person who was lying down, so that he would take more care of the body than was necessary.

Hence, when some people who were of the same mind and opinion considered his labors, they referred to him to build one dwelling for all. For those who are now scattered said more exactly and accurately that they would live, and that he would be free from a great part of anxiety. A very wise man proved the plan, and when he had forced them all together, and had pulled down those little houses, and had built one for those who were gathered together, he asked them to live together and encourage one another. and another, sharing the vigils, should receive the discipline of fasting. For thus, he says, by taking from one another what is lacking, we shall produce the most perfect virtue. For how, outside the states, one person sells bread, and another sells vegetables; another has clothes for sale, another is a shoemaker; but by obtaining from each other what they need, they lead a more pleasant life; for he who gives clothes receives shoes for them; but he who buys vegetables sells bread: thus we must exchange with each other the most precious parts of virtue. When those who were of the same language exercised and contended in this way, and praised God in the Greek voice, the love of this institution of life also took hold of those who used the language of that region. and some, coming together, begged that they too might be admitted into their flock, and that they might be partakers of its sacred doctrine. And he granted what they demanded, remembering the law of Sunday which he gave to the holy apostles, saying: Go and teach all nations (Matthew 28). And when he had built another abode next to that, he ordered them to dwell there, having built a kind of divine temple, in which he ordered both these and those to assemble, at the beginning of the day and at the end: that they might offer the evening and morning hymns to God at the same time, divided indeed into two parts, and each in his own using the voice, and sending out a song in succession. But the form of his institution has continued to this day, and neither has the time since he strove vehemently to change these things; nor those who succeeded in his treatment, so as to overturn something from the limits set by him, bring to mind; and that when not two or three, but many, had undertaken this governorship. For when he had first fulfilled the struggle, and had passed from this life, and migrated into it empty of all trouble, Theotecnus indeed received the governorship of the Greek language, and Aphthonius of Syria, who were to both of them certain animated statutes and images of that virtue. For neither those who assembled together, nor those who came from without, consented to have any sense of that death, so that those who had been instituted by that life should show themselves the likenesses expressed. But the godlike Theotecnus, having not lived long, handed over the governorship to Theodotus: but Aphthonius, taking care of the flock, and ruling by the laws which had already been passed, continued for a very long time. And this Thodotus, a native of Armenia, when he had seen that order of monastic training, was indeed the first in the number of those who appeared to the great governor Theotecnus; it was almost dark. For in such a way the divine desire affected him, and afflicted him with so many and such arrows, that he shed tears of remorse by night and by day. And he was so full of spiritual grace, that while he was praying, all who were present were indeed silent, but only heard those sacred words, clearly leading that hearing to a good prayer. For who would have been so adamantine, that those words spoken so sincerely and earnestly, would not soften his soul, and soften his hardness and disobedience, and transfer him to the service of God? When he thus daily increased his riches and showed the sacred treasures full of such good things, after he had fed the flock for twenty-five years, he was added to his fathers, as the divine Scripture says (Gen. A brother's son, but a brother in character.

Now, however, the divine Aphthonius, too, having presided over the choir for more than forty years, took the priestly seat; He was also fed with the same food as his ancestors before he was born. Moreover, even though he had received this treatment, he took care of that flock in no other way, spending many days there: and now, indeed, settling the disputes of those who were fighting among themselves, now, however, advising them who were affected by some injury; sometimes, however, extending a divine admonition to the members. And he was doing each of these things, either sewing cloths for his roommates, or cleaning the lens, or washing the corn, or handling something of the like. And when he had thus adorned the priesthood, and increased his power, he arrived at the divine harbor with his burdens.

And what need be said of Theotecnus, and of Gregory, who followed him, of whom indeed from his youth he gathered every kind of virtue and surpassed the glory of his ancestors; but here he still labors to this day in a deep old age, just as if he were in the prime of his life. For he continued continually refusing the fruit of the vine, and eating neither vinegar nor grapes, nor milk, nor fresh, nor concrete. For Publius the Great was determined to live thus: but recognizing the use of oil at the time of Pentecost, they again refuse to be partakers of it. These things I learned of the great Publius, which I received in part by hearsay, but in part from the very disciples whom I saw in them, in whom I recognized the teacher, and I learned the trifle through the athletes.

Thinking therefore that it was unjust, and of a man of the world, to enjoin so much advantage in silence, I proposed to those who did not know the narrative, that they might also take advantage of it, and thereby prepare the gain of memory for me. For I heard the Lord say: Whosoever shall confess me before men, I will also confess him before my Father which is in heaven (Matt. 10) and I know clearly that if I make a memory of them among men, it will happen that they will also remember me with the God of all.

CHAPTER VI: SIMEON THE OLD

But if anyone deliberately omits the old Simeon (Theodor., lib. iv. Hist., c. 26), and orders the memory of his philosophy to be forgotten, he may be justly accused of injury and envy, so that he does not want to praise those things which are worthy of praise, nor those let those who wish to be helped propose those things which are most to be desired. But I, not fearing to accuse, but desiring to pursue him with praise, I will relate the institution of his life.

For a very long time he embraced a solitary life, and living in a small cave, no human soul enjoyed it, for he had decided to live alone; but he talked constantly with the God of the universe, and he prepared edible herbs for his food, in which his labor was consumed. And from above he had been given such abundant grace, that he commanded even the strongest and most daring beasts. And this became evident not only to the pious, but also to the unbelieving Jews. For when, on account of some business of theirs, he set out abroad to a certain fort which was situated outside the country inhabited by the men of our empire, and a heavy rain arose and a storm fell, they indeed strayed from the road, so that those in front could not see them. finding neither a village, nor a cave, nor any traveler. But when they were tossed about by the waves in the midst of the continent, as those who sail in the middle of the waves, they noticed the cave of the divine Simeon, as it were a certain port, and beheld a dirty and squalid man, and a certain scanty cloth woven of goat's skin upon his shoulders. But as soon as he saw them, he greeted them (for he was amiable) and asked them the reason for their coming. And when they had told them what had happened, and asked him to show them the way that led to the fort, he said, Stay, I will immediately give you guides who will show you the way you desire. And indeed, they then prepared and rested. And to those who were sitting, two lions approached, not staring fiercely and fiercely, but as if flattering a certain master, and signifying servitude. Nodding to them, he ordered them to lead the guests and bring them back to the road from which they had strayed. But no one will think that a narrative is fabulous, since it has common enemies of the truth bearing witness to the truth; for they themselves, having obtained a boon, chanted this continually; and this the great James told me, saying that he was present when they told this miracle to blessed Maron. He, then, who does not believe the Jews bearing witness to the miracles of the Christians, how shall he not rightly be called more unbelieving than the Jews? Indeed, even if they are hostile towards us, they are nevertheless conquered and yield to the rays of truth; but these, since they are considered benevolent and partners in the faith, do not even believe the enemies who testify to the power of grace. But when that divine man had escaped, distinguished by such miracles, and had attracted many of the barbarous neighbors (who inhabit that wilderness who boast of Ishmael as the founder of the race), loving rest, he had to leave the cave. And when he had gone a long way, he came to a mountain which is called Amanus; and that which was formerly filled with the madness of the worship of many gods, he cultivated with many miracles of every kind, and planted the piety and true religion which is now practiced in it.

But it would indeed be very laborious to tell everything, and perhaps it could not be done by me at all. When, therefore, I have made mention of one, and have added, as it were, a certain form and character of an apostolic and prophetic miracle, I leave it to the readers to consider whose power of grace he received.

It was summer, and the harvest, and the teams were being driven into the fields. Now a certain man, who was not just content with his own labors, but lusted after another's, had indeed taken some of his neighbor's sheaves, and by these means he was trying to increase his wealth: but at once the divine judgment was passed upon his theft; lightning fell, and the ground was scorched. But that miserable man approached the man of God, who had pitched a tent not far from the village; and what had indeed befallen him, he recounted the calamity, but tried to conceal the theft. But after he had been commanded to tell the truth, he had confessed the theft (for he was compelled by chance to accuse himself), he commanded that divine man to correct the wrong he had done in order to be freed from punishment. For if you, he says, loose those bands, that fire sent by God will be extinguished; therefore, it was permitted to see him indeed running, and offering the ears stolen by theft to him to whom the injury had been done, and the pyre extinguished without water, by the prayer and intercession of the divine old man. This not only filled the inhabitants with terror, but also compelled the whole city, I say Antioch (for this estate was in his domain), to run thither, and to ask one to be delivered from the demoniacal rage, another to be relieved of the fever, and another to be of some of those who they tortured him in order to obtain a remedy. He, on the other hand, abundantly supplied those who dwelt with streams of grace.

But again, loving rest, he wanted to reach Mount Sinai. Now when many excellent men, who were pursuing the same philosophy, knew this, they ran together, desiring to be companions in his pilgrimage. And when they had completed a journey of many days, after they had come to the wilderness of Sodom, they saw in the distance the hands of men which were stretched out from the depths to the depths. And at first, they thought that it was a trick of the devil; but when they had prayed with greater earnestness of mind, and had seen the same, they proceeded to that place, and indeed saw a small trench, such as foxes are wont to make, when they plot what they are going through; but they saw none appear there. For when he heard the noise of the feet of him who had outstretched hands, he hid himself inside the cave. But the old man, having stayed a long time, begged very much that he would show himself to him if he had a human nature, and was not an impostor, some demon, who would change himself into these forms. Indeed, he says, we too, pursuing the life of monastic training, and loving rest, wander through this wilderness, desiring to worship the God of all on Mount Sinai, in whom he appeared to his servant Moses, and gave the tablets of the laws; not that we think that God is limited by place; for we hear him saying: I fill heaven and earth, says the Lord (Jer. 23); and that it contains the environment of the earth, and those who dwell in it like locusts: but since those who love ardently do not only long for those they love, but also for them are pleasant and pleasant places in which they have been present and in which they have been engaged. When the old man was saying these and similar things, the man who had been hiding in it appeared from the cave. He was indeed of a wild appearance, with scruffy hair, a wrinkled face, and all the limbs of his body were dried up and completely drained of blood. And he was clothed in some dirty cloths, made of palm branches. And when he had saluted, and given the word of peace, he asked who they were, and whence they came, and whither they were going. And he answered the question, and in turn asked whence he came, and why he had chosen this life. In the same way, he said, I had also begun to desire to go where you are now going but for this life I had assumed a certain relative of mine, and who was of the same mind and opinion, and who was the same as my goal and institution. But let us bind ourselves to one another by swearing, not even by death to separate our custom. It happened, therefore, that he, indeed, in his pilgrimage, took the end of his life here. But I, being bound by the oath, made a trench as best I could, and delivered the body to the burial: for this reason, having dug a second grave for me, I await the end of my life here, and I offer the usual service to the Lord. But I am eating dactyls, which a certain brother has been ordered to bring to me by him who is in charge. When these things were thus said, a lion appeared at a distance. But when those who were with the old man had fallen down with anguish and fear, he who was lying in the cave, feeling it, got up and beckoned to the lion to pass to another side. And he gave birth immediately, and came, bringing a bunch of dactyls. Then he went away again when he had been given permission and lying down far from the men he fell asleep. When, therefore, he had distributed the dactyls to all, and had shared in their prayers and psalms, and after the end of the morning service he had saluted them, he dismissed them, amazed at the novelty of the spectacle.

But if anyone has no faith in what has been said, let him remember the remarkable life of Elijah, and the ministry of the ravens, which indeed brought him bread in the morning, but flesh in the evening; for it is easy for the creator of the universe to find every way to provide for his own. Thus, he kept Jonah in the whale's belly for three days and nights and caused the lions in the lake to astonish Daniel, and for the empty fire to work as if endowed with reason, and indeed to illuminate those who were within, but to burn those who were without. But for I am doing a superfluous thing, who bring evidence to prove the power of God.

After he had reached the mountain which he longed for, they say that the admirable old man, in that place in which Moses is worthy to see God (and he saw that he could be seen by human nature), bowed his knees, and did not rise until he heard the divine voice which spoke to him. it signified the benevolence of the Lord. But since he had been so perpetually bent over the whole week, and had not taken the least bit of food, the voice which came to him commanded him to take what was set before him, and to eat with a prompt and eager heart. And when he had stretched out his hand, and found three evils, and had eaten them, as the one who had given them had commanded, his strength was restored to him, and he greeted those who were with him with a cheerful spirit, as was his match. He therefore returned happy and cheerful, as if he had heard the divine voice and had again eaten the food given by God.

On his return, he built two gymnasiums of philosophy: one indeed on the top of the mountain, of which we spoke before; and the other below, because of the very edges of the side of the mountain. But when he had assembled athletes of valor in both, he was the trainer of both of these and of them. And teaching insults to the adversary, and promising benevolence to the contestants, and commanding them to be of a good mind, but not to be degenerate and small-minded, and commanding them to use moderation in their own, but in the enemy to use greatness of mind, teaching these things, living thus, doing these miracles, and the splendor of every kind sending forth, took the end of this laborious life, and passed away into that which is old age and trouble, leaving behind a glory which cannot be extinguished, and a memory which remains forever the blessing of Him, while he was still alive, blessed, and so thrice blessed, mother she obtained mine, and often told me many things about it.

But now I pray that I may obtain his intercession as much as he can give; and I know that he will succeed me: for he will completely grant the request, imitating the kindness of the Lord.

CHAPTER VII: PALLADIUS

But Palladius, who was celebrated in the speech of many (Theodor., lib. iv. Hist., ch. 26), and was equal to him in time, and similar in manners, and familiar and familiar. For, as they say, they fanned each other, took advantage of each other, provoked each other, and incited them to the jealousy of God. Now he was shut up in a certain little house, which was near the largest village and the most populous by far: and his name is 'Iemme'. And I think it is unnecessary to say that the most important thing for a man is abstinence from food, or fasting and hunger, and vigilance, and perpetual prayer. For in these he drew the same yoke as the blessed Simeon. But the miracle which is sung to this day, was done by his voice and hand, I thought that if I told it I would make it worthwhile.

In the aforesaid village a most famous assembly takes place, which attracts merchants from all quarters, and a greater multitude than can be enumerated. In it a certain merchant, having sold what he had brought, and having forced gold, wished to retire at night. And a certain murderer, who had looked at the gold collected there, struck with a sort of anger and fury, indeed wiped away sleep from his eyelashes, but watched when that man was about to depart. But after the crowing of the rooster, he indeed went away in safety; but this one, coming in advance, when he had occupied a certain place suitable for ambushes, suddenly fell upon him, and struck him down and made a slaughter. But by cursing the wicked, he also added another deed; for when he had taken the gold, he threw that dead body at the door of Palladius. But when the day had come, and the report had spread, and the whole assembly of men was talking here and there about what had happened, they all came together, and breaking open the door, they wanted to demand from the divine Palladius the punishment for the murder that had been committed. he had committed a murder. When, therefore, the divine man was surrounded by such a multitude, looking at the heavens, and surpassing the heavens in his mind, he besought the Lord to refute the lie of the slander, and to show the truth which was hidden. When he had thus prayed, and had taken the hand of the lying man, he said, "Say, O youth, who has inflicted this wound upon thee: show me who has committed this accursed deed and deliver the innocent from this impious calumny." But the speech was indeed followed by a speech. And the man sitting on the right hand was indeed looking around at those who were approaching, but he was pointing his finger at the murderer. A cry was raised from all, and those who marveled at the miracle, and lamented the slander that had been intended. But when they had undressed that criminal, they found the sword still bleeding with blood, and the gold which had given the cause of the murder. But the divine Palladius, since he had been admirable before, now became by merit far more admirable. For a miracle was sufficient to show the man's trust in God.

Of the same order was also the admirable Abraham, who indeed built what is called Parathomon, and sent forth the splendors of his power in every direction. The miracles that took place after his death testify to how bright his life was. Cures of all kinds of diseases spring from his tomb to this day. And of this there are rich witnesses, who draw them abundantly from the other side by faith. But it is given to me also to obtain the help that I have sanctified the language in memory of them.

CHAPTER VIII: APHRAATES

That the nature of all men is one, and that it is easy for those who wish to philosophize, whether they be Greeks or barbarians, is readily known from many others; but for this to be clearly shown even Aphraates alone is sufficient (Theodor., lib. IV Hist., chap. 24). For among the Persians, who are the most unjust, and born and brought up, and born of such parents, and raised in their laws, he attained to such prowess, that he obscured those who were born of the pious and had received pious instruction from an early age. For at first, despised by his race (and it was a clear and illustrious one), he ran to worship the Lord, he imitated his elders, the magicians, then, abhorred by the impiety of men of his own race, he preferred a foreign country to his own. And when he came to Edessa (it is the largest city and the most populous, and which is markedly adorned with piety), when he found a little house outside its borders, and shut himself up in it, he took care of his soul, like a certain good husbandman, cutting out the thorns of vices by the root, and divine clearing the crop, and offering the ripe fruits of the Gospel to the Lord. From there he came to Antioch, which was severely besieged by heretical storms, where, having previously converted the city into a kind of gymnasium of philosophy, and having learned a few words of the Greek language, he drew many to hear the divine discourses: receiving this flow of the divine Spirit. For who among those who flaunt their eloquence, and contract their brows and speak loudly and magnificently, and exult youthfully because of the snares of syllogisms, was ever superior to that unlearned and barbarous voice? For he overcame the reasonings of the philosophers with his reasonings, and with the divine speeches of the philosophers, crying out with the great Paul, though unskilled in speech, yet not in knowledge (2 Cor. 11). But in this way, he continually, according to the apostle's opinion, lowered the reasons, and all the height which is exalted against the knowledge of God, and captivated all intelligence to the obedience of Christ (2 Cor. 10). Now it was permitted to see those who carried the magistrates, and those who were enrolled in certain numbers of the militia, and those who procured their food by hand; and let me say once, both the private and the soldiers, and the learned, and the unlettered, and the poor, and the rich; But when he took so much labor, he never suffered to take any one to live with him; He preferred his own work to the service and service offered to him by others. And when his meetings and conversations took place at the gate of the court, he himself opened it for those who entered, and led in and dismissed those who departed. But he never received anything at all from anyone, not bread, not food, not clothes, but only one person known to him supplied him with bread. But when the old man had gone down to the depths, after sunset he was feeding on vegetables.

And they say that Anthemius, who afterwards was both governor and consul, when he was elected ambassador went to the Persians, brought to him a tunic woven by the Persians, and said: When I knew that every man had his own sweet country, and that the fruits that grow there are the most pleasant, this from his country I have brought you a coat, and I ask you to accept it, but I will be a partaker of your blessing. And he indeed first ordered her to be placed in the seat; then, when many conversations had been interrupted, he said that he was troubled in mind, as if his thought was divided into two parts; And when he asked the reason, he said, I have always decided to have only one person to live with me. and I imposed this law on myself, so that the habitation of two people at the same time would be completely denied to me. When, therefore, one had already lived with me for sixteen years, and was dear to me, a fellow-citizen of mine came, desiring to live with me, and begging that this might be permitted to him. This distracts my mind, for I will not allow myself to have two at the same time. For I embrace the contributor to contribute; but to expel the former, as one who was dear to my heart, I consider both grave and unjust. But he said: I deserve it, O Father, for it is not right that you should love him who has served you most of the time, as if he were not fit; but he whose behavior you have not yet made a danger to, for the sole sake of admitting your country. To these the divine Aphraates: I will not accept, then, O man of wonder, this coat; for I will not suffer to have two. For my opinion is indeed more agreeable, and yours is better than that which has served me so long. When he thus outwitted Anthemius by a clever remark, and exhibited a miracle of great skill, he persuaded that no one should deal with him henceforth in regard to that coat. I have reported these things, wishing to show two things at once: and that he received from one person alone what was sufficient for the care of the body, and that his wisdom was so great that he made it so that whoever asked him to receive it, gave the opinion that he should not receive it. But leaving these and things of this kind, I will tell the greater things.

When Julianus, hostile to God, had inflicted punishments on impiety in the country of the barbarians, things were indeed for a little while calmer for the students of piety, when Jovinianus had received the helm of the Roman empire; ours was driven about, and a heavy wave was raised, and the greatest waves attacked the boat on every side. But the storm was made worse by the solitude of the pilots. For the emperor, who was exercising audacity in his only true religion, forced them to live in exile. And since his use of iniquity was so great, he was not satisfied with impiety, but dispersed and dispersed the assembly of all the pious, like a wild beast striving to tear a herd. For this reason, he not only expelled them from every church, but also from the side of the mountain, and from the bank of the river, and from the military gymnasium.

PHILOTHEUS OR THEOPHILOS

For these places were constantly changing, so that the armed hand might suddenly rage against them. And the Scythians, indeed, and other barbarians, securely populated the whole of Thrace from the Danube to the Propontis; but he used arms against those who were of the same race, and of his domain, and of fame in piety and religion. And the divine people of those evils lamented the importunity, singing that Davidic song: We sat there upon the rivers of Babylon; and we wept while we remembered you, O Zion (Ps. 136). But the rest of the songs did not suit them. For Aphraates, and Flavianus, and Diodorus, did not allow the instruments of doctrine to be hung up in the willows; nor did they suffer to say: How shall we sing the song of the Lord in a foreign land (Ps. 136)? But in the mountains, and in the fields, and in the city, and in the suburbs, and in the houses, and in the streets, they sang the song of the Lord constantly. For they had learned from David, the earth is the Lord's, and the fullness of it, the world of the earth, and all who dwell in it (Ps. 23). Again, they had heard the same Prophet crying: Bless the Lord, all his works, in every place of his dominion (Ps. 22). And they also heard the divine Paul commanding men to pray in every place, lifting up holy hands without anger and disputing (1 Tim. 2). Moreover, the Lord himself, speaking with the Samaritan woman, foretold this more openly: For, he said, I say to you, woman, the hour is coming, and now is, when neither in this place, nor in Jerusalem, but in every place, they will worship the Father (John 5). When they had learned these things, both in the house and in the market, and, as I may say apostolically, they were constantly testifying publicly and through houses (Acts 20); and like some of the most distinguished emperors, they indeed armed their own men, but stabbed their adversaries. And indeed the great Flavian and the divine Theodore, who at that time fed under another, and were considered worthy of the second chair, did these things which I have said, and indeed it is admirable, and worthy of praise: but still they did these things, when they were elected commanders of the army, and subject to the laws imperial Aphraates, the wisest of all, of his own free will leapt into these contests; for he was brought up in peace, and when it was his policy to live by himself, and to sit out of range of the weapon, as it is said, when he saw the fierceness of the war, he did not like that he should be safe, but commanding peace to be strong for a time, he was the leader of the pious phalanx in the battle, striking indeed, both by life and speech and miracles, but he himself was never struck. Quinetes, when the emperor, being in every respect a fool, had once seen him going out to the military gymnasium (for it happened that then there were assembled there those who were properly venerable members of the Trinity), but someone pointing him out to the emperor who was walking on the bank of the river, asked him where he was going. And when he had said that he was going to plead for the world and for the empire, the emperor again answered: And for what reason, having professed the monastic life, do you enter safely through the forum, left in silence and quiet? And he (for he used to imitate the Lord, to reason parabolically): Tell me, said the emperor, if I were a virgin sitting in the chamber, and I saw someone throwing fire into my father's house, what would you advise me to do, seeing the flame burning, and the house that is burning, inside? to sit and look down upon the house which is burning? But I too would have been consumed by the fire. But if you say that it is necessary to hasten, to bring water, and to run after it, and to extinguish the flame; Do not blame me, O Emperor, if I do the same thing. For what you advise the virgin who is in the chamber, this I am compelled to do, who have professed the monastic life. But if you blame me for leaving the rest, blame yourself for throwing this flame into the divine house; and not me, who am trying to extinguish it. For it is necessary to bring help to the father's house which is burning, you will also confess. Now that God is a truer and truer Father than those who are on earth is open to everyone, even those who are not at all initiated into divine things. Therefore, O emperor, we do nothing absurd, nor contrary to our beginning and our institution, if we gather together and feed the disciples of the true religion, and present to them the divine herb. With these words, the emperor indeed tacitly agreed, considering it a just defense.

Now one of those who are considered neither men nor women, but the possibility of ever becoming fathers has been taken away from them, and for this reason they are considered to be well-wishing for the emperor and to speak confidently to him, he from a higher place was accused of insulting the divine man, and threatened with death; but not so long after the punishment of his audacity. For when the emperor wanted to wash his body in the bath, the wretch actually approached the couch as if to see whether it was properly tempered, but his mind was seized, and he jumped into the couch, which contained hot water not at all tempered; and when no one was present inside (for he had entered alone, he was going to see if he was ready) he remained cooked and resolved. And when the time was spent in the meantime, the emperor sent another to call him: and when he found no one in that house, he reported it to the emperor. But when then many had run, searching all the steps, and had at last come to it, they saw him lying and deprived of life. But when there was a tumult, and all were fainting, some indeed drained the hot water, while others lifted up the miserable body. Hence it came to pass that fear invaded the emperor and all who were armed against piety. Now the report was spread throughout the whole city, how that unfortunate man had suffered the punishments of the insult he had inflicted on Aphraates, and all celebrated the god of Aphraates with perpetual praises. This, even though the adversaries insisted, prevented the man of God from being sent into exile. For the emperor, terrified, turned away from those who suggested these things, but respected the man.

Moreover, he also learned his virtue from another source. A certain horse, born of a good breed, and very learned to carry, was very dear to the emperor: a certain disease which had befallen him afflicted the emperor badly, and the excretion of wet excrement was kept up; those who had been trained in this art were gathered to take care of him. But when she was also inferior to the disease, the emperor was indeed affected by the trouble; but he was lamenting to whom the care of the horses had been entrusted. But when he was pious and firm in faith, he came at noon with his horse to the abode of the great Aphraates; and when he had spoken of his illness, and had signified his faith, he prayed that he might relieve the illness by his prayers. But he did not hesitate, but at once prayed to God, and ordered water to be drawn from the well; and when the savior had made the sign of the cross upon her, he ordered her to be brought to the horse: but he drank more than he was wont to do. Then, when he had filled the oil with a divine invocation and blessing, he anointed the horse's belly, and with the contraction of his hands the disease was immediately removed. The happy man, therefore, having received the horse, ran to the stable. And in the evening (for at that time the emperor was wont to come to the stable) he came and asked how the horse was doing. And when he had signified that he was healthy, and had brought out a strong horse, exulting, neighing, and raising his neck proudly, he asked him the cause of his health. But when he hesitated for a long time (for he was afraid to show the doctor, knowing that he who asked him was angry with him), he was finally forced to tell the truth, and taught the method of treatment. The emperor was indeed amazed, and confessed that he was an admirable man, and yet his madness did not cease from the former, but went on raging against the Only begotten, until he was consumed by fire by the barbarian, not even deigning to be buried with servants or beggars. And the divine Aphraates showed his prowess even in that storm, and he also did the same with calmness. Moreover, he also performed other innumerable miracles, of which I remember one or two.

A certain woman of noble birth, at the same time pulling the yoke of matrimony with an intemperate husband, came to that blessed man, lamenting her own calamity. For he said that the husband of his concubine had been taken by habit, had been bewitched by certain magical tricks, and hated that she was lawfully wedded. And these things said the woman standing before the doors of the court; for thus the woman used to speak to him, for he never admitted anyone within the doors. Then, therefore, the woman, weeping for pity, abrogates the operation by a prayer of incantation: and when she had sanctified the drop of oil which she had brought by divine invocation, she commanded that it should be anointed with it. When the woman had fulfilled these precepts, she transferred the love of the couple into herself, and persuaded him to choose a legitimate bed instead of an illegitimate one.

Now they also say that when the locusts once suddenly invaded the country and consumed everything like fire, crops, trees, meadows and groves, a certain pious man came to him, asking him to bring help to a man who had one piece of land, and from it both himself and his wife and to support his children and family, and from whom also an imperial contribution was demanded. He, therefore, again imitating the kindness of the Lord, ordered a bowl of water to be brought to him. And after he had brought a bowl of water, he who was praying laid his hand on him; And he prayed to God to fill the stream with divine power, then, having finished his prayer, he ordered that water be sprinkled on the borders of the farm. He who had brought it did as he had been commanded, and that was for those fields as a sacrosanct and impregnable rampart; for the locusts crawling and circling as far as those borders, like an army, retreated again, fearing the benediction which had been imposed upon them, and being suffocated, as it were, by a kind of bridle, and forbidden to advance further.

And what need is to be said of all that was done by that blessed soul? for these things are sufficient to show the splendor of the grace which dwelt in him.

I saw him, and received the blessing of his holy right hand, when I was indeed still a youth, and I had joined my mother in my departure for him. And when, as was his custom, he opened the door, he graced it with his speech and a blessing; Let me enjoy it now, too, so that those who believe that he lives, and lead choirs together with the angels, and use greater confidence in God than before. For it was then measured by the mortal body, that the occasion of arrogance might not escape, if it had been greater than its equal confidence. But now I lay aside the burden of mental disorders, as the athlete, having won victory, uses confidence and the ability to speak freely with the athlete. For this reason, I also pray that I may obtain his intercession.

CHAPTER IX: PETER

Indeed, we hear of the Gauls who are in Europe to the West (Theodor., book IV Hist., chap. 26). And we also know that those who are in Asia are descended from those who established settlements on account of Pontus Euxine. From them sprouted the blessed Peter, and so the three and four blessed ones. But seven years, as they say, after he was born, brought up by his parents, he spent all the rest of his life in the struggles of philosophy. It is said that he died when he had lived ninety-nine years.

Who then praised him for his dignity, who contended for ninety-two years, and was always victorious at night and for a long time? And what language was sufficient for him to narrate the things that he had done brilliantly and with valor, in childhood and youth, in manhood and growing old, and in extreme old age? Who measured that sweat? Who has enumerated the struggles which have taken place in so long a time? But what kind of prayer could the seeds sown by him, or the sheaves gathered, achieve? Who is endowed with such a great and lofty mind as to be able to look perfectly at the resources and forces gathered from a splendid trade? I know the vastness of the events of that event, and therefore I am afraid to proceed to tell the story, lest the speech be overwhelmed. Therefore, I will walk for the sake of the shore, and what has happened on the mainland, I will marvel and tell before the sea, but I will leave the deep to him who, as the divine Scripture says, searches the deep and knows the hidden things (1 Cor. 2; Dan. 2).

Here, therefore, at the first time he fought in Galatia, thence he came to Palestine with the grace of seeing, that when he saw the places which had received salutary sufferings, he might in them worship God who saved him; not that he should be circumscribed in a place (for he knew that his nature could not be circumscribed), but that he might feed his eyes with the spectacle of what is desired; nor would the soul's strength alone, which is contemplated, without sight, enjoy spiritual nourishment through faith. For those who pursue someone with love, it is innate by nature that they take pleasure not only from the sight of him, but also to contemplate the house and clothes and shoes with great joy. The bride, endowed with love for such a bridegroom, who yearned in the Song of Songs, cried out, saying: As evil is in the trees of the forest, so is my cousin in the midst of children. I longed and sat in his shadow, and his sweet fruit in my throat (Cant. 2). This divine man, therefore, did nothing absurd and strange, who indeed took the same love as his bridegroom, and used the same words as his bride: I am wounded, he cried, by love (Cant. 4). But when he longed to behold the bridegroom as a certain shadow, he went to see the places from which the fountains of salvation for all men flowed.

When, therefore, he had been permitted to enjoy what he desired, he indeed set out for Antioch, the same yoke of piety and religion. When he had decided to stay there, he did not pitch a tent, he did not fix a hut, he did not raise a small house, but spent the whole time in someone else's tomb. In it, however, there was a projection of a certain upper story, to which a staircase connected, received those who wished to ascend. He remained shut up in it for a very long time, indeed using warm water, but eating only bread, and that not every day, but once, indeed, remaining fast, and taking it the next day.

But when a certain man, maddened and stricken with rage, and full of the work of an evil demon, came to him, he indeed cleansed him, supplicated him, and delivered him from that diabolical fury. When he would not go away but begged him to impart his service to him in exchange for that treatment, he admitted him to live with him. I knew him, and I remember the miracles, and I saw the reward of healing, and I heard the conversation they had about me. For Daniel (for this was his name) said that I, too, would be a future partner in this illustrious ministry. But that divine man did not agree that this should be done, considering the love of my parents for me; but he often fed me with grapes and bread laid on his knees. For when my mother had made a spiritual danger of his grace, she ordered me to reap his blessing once a week. And he had knowledge of this cause: the disease which had lain in one of his eyes, seemed to overcome the knowledge of medicine; for there was nothing either written by the ancients, or discovered by those who came later, that was not used by disease. But after he had tried everything, and shown that it was of no use, there came to him a certain relative who showed him a divine man and taught him a miracle wrought by him. For he said that his wife, who at that time held the scepter of the administration of the East (and that was Pergamene), when she fell into this disease, she herself cured him by the use of supplication and the sign of the cross. The mother heard it, and immediately ran to the divine man: but he had earrings, chains, and necklaces, and other gold which he had put on, and a garment of various colors woven from silk threads: for he had not yet tasted a more perfect power; but she flourished in time and wore the world of a woman as a young girl. When, therefore, she had looked upon the divine head, she cured the first disease of excessive adornment of love, using such words as these: Tell me, she said, daughter (for I will use her voice, and I will not change the word of that holy tongue), if any painter, well trained in the art, had painted any a picture, as the law of art dictates, and he had proposed it to those who wished to see it; then, criticizing that artificial painting, he would indeed add longer lines to the eyebrows and eyelashes, and make the face whiter, and add a red color to the cheeks; Does it not seem to you that the former painter would be rightly indignant, because his art was both disgraceful and affected by insults, and he had received additions from an uneducated hand of those for whom he had no need? Therefore, he says, believe the workman of the universe, and the maker and painter of our nature, to be rightly angry, because that which cannot be explained in words, nature and wisdom, you have accused of ignorance. For you will not infuse yourself with red and white and black colors, if you do not think that you need this addition. But those who think that they need the body, the creator of infirmity, is condemned. But it must be known that he has a power corresponding to his will in just symmetry. For, as David said, the Lord did all that he willed (Ps. 113, 134). But what is good for all, and taking care of the future, does not give those things which bring harm. Therefore, do not corrupt the image of God, nor attempt to add those things which He has not wisely given, nor with this adulterous invention beauty, which brings destruction even to the chaste, by lying in wait for those who see it. A very excellent and in every way the best woman heard this, and immediately she was entangled in Peter's net (for he was also caught in the same way, and he who had the same name as himself), and touching his feet, and crying out, begged him to take care of his eye. But he said that he was indeed a man, and that he had the same nature as himself; but that he should bear a great burden of sins, and therefore be deprived of that which is held in trust in God. But when the mother wept and prayed and said that she would not leave him unless he obtained health, he said that God was their guardian, and that he would always give requests to those who believe. He will give, he says, now also, not giving me grace, but contemplating your faith. If, then, you have it sincere and true, pure and free from all doubt, commanding both physicians to heal and medicines, take this medicine given by God. When he had said these things, he laid his hand on his eye, and, making the sign of the saving cross, expelled the disease. Returning home from there, when she had washed off the medicine, and thrown away all adornment introduced from without, she instituted her life according to the laws laid down by the physician: neither dressed in various clothes, nor adorned with gold necklaces, and this, since she was still very young in age; for she was born in the twenty-third year, and had not yet become a mother: for when she had lived another seven years, she gave birth to me, who was her first and only child. He received so much fruit from the teaching of the great Peter, and he received a double treatment; and when he sought medicine for the body, he also prepared for himself a good condition for the soul. By saying such things, he worked, and he was so powerful in praying.

And when she had once brought a cook's servant, who was tormented by an evil demon, she begged him not to refuse her help. When the divine man had been prayed for, he commanded the demon to tell him the reason why he had power over God's creature. And he, like a murderer, or a wall-piercer, and a robber, standing before the judge, and commanded to tell what he had done, was thus persecuted in all things, as if he were compelled to tell the truth out of custom; and he said to Heliopolis that the master of the servant was indeed ill; and the lady of the couple, as being sick, sat down; and to the handmaids of the lady of the house in which they were staying, she told of the life of the monks who philosophized in Antioch, and what strength they had against demons; and these indeed, as girls, delighted in the game, acted demoniacally and madly; and that servant himself, clothed in a monastic garment made of goat's skin, had sworn them monastically. When these things were done, he said, I, standing before the doors, and not bearing those proud and glorious things which were said of the monks, I wanted to make a danger of the power which they youthfully boasted of having. For this reason, leaving the handmaids, I entered this place, desiring to know how I should be expelled from the monks. But now, said he, "I have learned, and need no other experience"; Saying these things, he fled, and the servant was freed.

Now, however, he had brought another peasant, who was indeed my mother's mother, but my aunt, and was begging the adversary of his vice to help him. And he asked again, where he was from, and from whom he had received power over God's creation. But as he remained silent and gave no answer, Peter bent his knees and prayed, and besought God to show him the power of his servants by cursing the demon. Then he rose again; but he resisted again, kept silent: and these things took place until the ninth hour. And after he had offered a prayer to the Lord with greater earnestness and more vehemence, he arose and said to the wicked demon: It is not Peter who commands you, but Peter's God. He has returned, even if he is an impudent, destructive demon, to the mildness and restraint of the saints; and with a loud voice, he cried out, that he was indeed engaged in the mountain of Amano. But when I saw him, says he, on the road, drawing and drinking water from some spring, I endeavored to take this abode for myself. But to go out, says the man of God, to him who was crucified for the world, commanding you this. He heard it, and fled, and in his fury the book was returned to the farmer. But while I could tell innumerable other things of this kind about that blessed soul, I will pass over most of them, fearing the weakness of the common people; for looking to themselves, they have no faith in the miracles of divine men. But when I have said one or two things, I will pass it on to another athlete.

There was a certain lustful man, who in former times had been a commander of the militia. And a certain girl, unmarried, but married, who was under his dominion, left her mother and her children, and fled to a certain gynaecium, in which was a group of athletes. For women also compete in the same way as men and descend to the stage of virtue. When the commander of the army learned of his flight, he fell to his mother with passion, and bound her, and did not release her from her chains until he showed her the dwelling of the religious women. And so, in his rage, he abducted the girl from there, and brought her back to his house; and the unhappy man hoped that he would satisfy his lust. But he who tempted Pharaoh with great and evil temptations concerning Sarah, Abraham's wife, and preserved the chaste woman untouched; and he who smote the Sodomites with blindness, who had attacked those who were incorporeal, as if they were guests, to be insulted with insults, when he had struck the courage of this living with blindness, he caused the prey to escape from his hands; He went out and disappeared from sight, and reached the most desirable dwelling. Thus, when the fool had learned that he would not overcome her who had chosen God as her spouse, he was forced to rest, no longer desiring her who had been captured and had escaped from the divine power. As this time progressed, he had fallen into a serious illness; but the disease was cancer, and when the breast was swollen the pain also increased. But he called Peter great, when he was in great pain; and he said, putting that sacred voice into his ears, that he was driven away by all the pain, and that he felt no sense of discomfort from thenceforth. For this reason, she was often comforted by him. For he said all that time that the pains of that presence had completely receded. But a certain one, when he had thus contended, pursued him, departing from this life with praises signifying his victory.

And again, my mother, when, after she had given birth to me, she was at the very gates of death, he came and rescued her from the hands of death, at the request of her aunt. For, as they say, he lay with the doctors despairing, but his relatives lamenting and awaiting the end, with his eyes closed, suffering from a violent fever, and recognizing none of his acquaintances. But after he had come who had been graced with apostolic speech and grace, and said, Peace to you, daughter (for this was his greeting), it is said that he immediately raised his eyelashes and looked at him with fixed eyes and gave him the fruit of the blessing. And after the chorus of women had howled (for their hearts were mingled with anguish and joy, and they were the cause of that shouting), the divine man commanded that they should all be partners in his prayer. For thus he said that even Tabitha had obtained salvation, indeed for weeping widows, but for the great Peter offering their tears to God (Acts 9). They prayed as he commanded and received as he foretold. For when the prayer came to an end, the disease also came to an end: and the sweat suddenly flowed from the whole body, and that fire was extinguished, and the signs of health appeared. God has done such miracles in our times through his benevolent servants.

The surface of this garment, too, was worked in the same way as that of the most divine Paul. Now I put this, not using any hyperbole, but agreeing to the truth that was said. For when he had divided his girdle into two parts (it was wide and long, woven of thick linen), he girded one half of this around his loins, and the other around mine. When my mother had often imposed this on me when she was sick, and often on my father also, she brought on the disease. Quintine herself, too, has often used this medicine for her health. And when many of his acquaintances had learned this, they constantly used this zone to help the sick, and everywhere the operation of that grace was shown. When someone thus received it, he deprived those who had given it, showing himself ungrateful to those who had done him the favor. In this way we were exposed to that gift. When he had thus shone, and lighted up Antioch with his rays, he was led away from the contests, awaiting the crown which is reserved for the victors.

But I, who, while he was still alive, perceived the blessing, and having prayed that I may enjoy it now also, I will put an end to this narrative.

CHAPTER XI: ROMANUS

Theodosius the Great, therefore, set out from Antioch, when he had fought in the Rosic mountains, and having returned to Antioch, he thus ended his life. And the divine Romanus, who was born in Rosi, and was first brought up in Antioch, showed the first contests of valor, indeed outside the city limits he fixed a tabernacle on the side of a mountain, but he lived all the time in a stranger's little house. But until he was old, he never used either fire or the light of a lamp. And his food was bread and salt; but the drink flowed from the fountain. And his hair was like the great Theodosius, and the garment of iron likewise.

Here, too, he abounded in simplicity of manners, meekness, and self-control, and therefore emitted the splendor of divine grace. Upon whom, he says, shall I look, but upon the gentle and quiet, and my trembling words (Is. 66)? But now again he also said to his disciples: Learn from me, for I am meek and lowly in heart, and you will find rest for your souls (Matt. 11). And again: Blessed are the meek, for they shall inherit the earth (Matt. 5). This was perhaps the most remarkable of Moses the lawgiver. For, he says, Moses was the meekest of all men who were upon the earth (Num. 12). The most holy Spirit also testified to this about the prophet David: "For remember, O Lord, David, and all his meekness" (Ps. 211). We also learned about the patriarch Jacob, that he was not a fake inhabitant of the house (Gen. 25). When he gathered these virtues like a bee from those divine meadows, he made the honey of true philosophy. But his most pleasant streams also deepened into the outsiders: and to those who came to him, using a gentle and sweet voice, he offered many admonitions about love for brothers, about concord and peace. And he made many lovers of divine things even with a single glance. For who would not have been astonished to a great extent, when he saw him afflicted in body, and who wore long hair, and carried the greatest weight of iron by himself, and wore clothes woven of hair, and took only enough food to prevent him from dying of hunger?

And to the greatness and multitude of his labors was added the grace which flourished in him, by which indeed all were persuaded to admire and honor him. For many times he caused severe diseases, and he obtained children from many barren women. And when he had received such power from the divine Spirit, he called himself a needy and a beggar. Therefore, as many as came to him, he filled them with usefulness, both in his sight and in his speech, during the whole time of his life.

Moreover, when he had passed from here also, and had been transferred to the angelic choir, he left behind a memory which was not buried together with the body, but which thrives, blossoms, and sprouts, and which cannot be extinguished, but always endures, and which is sufficient for those who will. helping them When, therefore, I have won a blessing for myself from here, I will tell the deeds of other athletes as well, as I can.

CHAPTER XII: ZENO.

Not many know the admirable Zeno; But those who know cannot be admired for their dignity (Theodore, book IV Hist., chapter 26). For when he had left the greatest riches in his country (and that was Pontus), great indeed, as he said, he drew the streams of Basilius, who was a neighbor, and irrigated the region of Cappadocia; For as soon as the emperor Valens had been removed from the midst, he laid down his military girdle: and he was enrolled in the number of those who speedily carried the emperor's letters. And when he had come from the king to a certain sepulcher (and there are many on the mountain) which is situated near Antioch, he dwelt there alone, purifying his soul, and always purifying his faculty of contemplation, and always grasping the divine contemplation with his vision, and arranging the ascent of God in his heart, and his feathers like a dove desiring to receive and to fly away into divine rest (Ps. 83; Ps. 55). For this reason, she had no bed, no lamp, no hearth, no pot, no drop, no bow, no book, and nothing else; but he was indeed clothed in old clothes, and his shoes were also of such a kind that they needed laces, for the leather of the soles was torn and torn. And from one of his relatives, he received the necessary food. Now that was one loaf of bread, which was supplied for two days; but drawing water at a distance, he carried it himself. But when anyone saw him carrying a burden, he asked him to lift it with labor. But he resisted at first; teaching that he could not bring himself to drink water which had been brought by another. But when he was not persuaded, he gave the urns; for he carried two in both hands: but when he was within the gate of the court, when he had poured out and dispersed the water, he ran again to the spring, confirming what he had said.

And I, too, when I first went up the mountain desiring to see him, I saw him holding urns in his hands. Then I asked him where the abode of the wonderful Zeno was. And he said that he knew no monk who was so called. But when I had conjectured that it was he, I followed, inferring this from the modesty of his speech. But after I had entered the door, I saw a bed made of hay, and a certain other store spread over the stones in such a way that those who sat on it were not in the least hurt by it. Now after we have spoken many words about philosophy; for I was asking questions, but he was explaining to us the things that were being asked: and it was then necessary to return home; I begged him to give a passage of blessing: but he resisted, saying that it was fair that we should fulfill the prayers, and indeed himself deprived, but calling us soldiers; for at that time I read the sacred books to the people of God. But when we brought forth youth and the immaturity of age (for then for the first time we produced a little wool of some sort) and swore that we would not come again if we were forced to do this, scarcely at last, indeed, after many bending prayers, he indeed offered an intercession to God; but that he had done so, he excused himself in many words, saying that he had done it both for the sake of love and obedience, for as we approached we heard him praying. But in so deep a philosophy, so modesty and moderate was the old man (for forty years he had been continually engaged in monastic training), who could be sufficiently admired for his dignity? But what praises could he bring equal to the greatness of the matter? But when he possessed such riches of virtue, as if he were in extreme poverty, he came to the church of God on Sundays with the people, listening to the divine discourses, and listening to the teachers; and after he had partaken of the mystical table, he returned to that new abode, having no key, no lock, and leaving no keeper: for it was completely inaccessible to the sorcerer and sacrosanct, so that he had only that store. And taking one book from his relatives, when he had read it all, and returning it first, he took another. But although he had neither barriers nor used bars, he was protected by divine grace; and this we have clearly learned by experience itself. For when the Isauri took the citadel by ambush at night, then in the morning they made incursions up to the side of the mountain, cruelly stabbing many men and many women who were practicing the monastic life; then the divine man, beholding the slaughter of the others, caused their eyes to be dimmed by prayer, and as they entered through the door, they could not see the way in. .

What kind of life, then, this divine man led, and what kind of grace he received from God, these things suffice to teach. But it is necessary to add this also to these. It grieved him greatly and he felt bad that his means had remained and had not been sold and distributed according to the evangelical law: and the cause of this was the immature age of the brothers. For as both money and possessions were in common, he indeed did not want to return to his country on account of division; but the others were afraid to sell a part of their resources, lest the buyers, moved by greed, limiting the brothers, should inflict disgrace upon them. Considering these things in his mind, he postponed the sale for a long time; but afterwards, when one of his acquaintances had sold everything, he indeed distributed most of it; meanwhile, bad health which had happened to him, compelled him to consult about the rest. And when he had come to the head of the city (and he was the great Alexander, the splendor of true religion, and the model of virtue, the exact and precise image of philosophy): Until now, he said, O divine head, you are the best financier of these funds for me, distributing them from the divine fund, as if you were a judge. He will give an account to him. For others I prepared with my own hand and distributed them as seemed to me the best; but since I am ordered to depart from this life, I appoint you as their administrator, who are also a priest, and you carry out the priestly office correctly according to the laws. He therefore handed over the money as if it were God's treasurer. But he himself, having lived no more than a year afterwards, retired from the fence like an Olympic victor, having obtained glory not only from men, but also from angels.

But I, having prayed to him to intercede for me with the Lord, will turn to another narrative.

CHAPTER XIII: MACEDONIUS

And the Macedonians, by the surname of Κριθοφάγον, that is, one who feeds on barley (for it was food that gave him this surname), are indeed known to all the Phoenicians and Syrians and Cylicians; and their neighbors and neighbors also know them, who partly saw the miracles themselves, and partly heard the fame celebrating them. . Nor indeed do they all know everything; but when some have indeed learned this, and others that, they are only astonished at what they know. As for me, when I shall know more perfectly to others about this divine head (for many things have moved me to go to him and to be frequent with him), I will tell as much detail as I can. But I kept this order for him, and after many, I placed his narrative, not that he was second to the others in virtue (for he was equal to the highest and the first), but that when he had lived a very long time, after those whom I remember, he ended his life.

Here, therefore, he had a gymnasium and a stadium, the tops of the mountains: he was not stationed in one place, but now indeed acting in this, now passing into that. And this he did, not carrying the places with difficulty, but fleeing the multitude of those who gathered to him, and who concurred from all sides. And for forty-five years he lived continually in this manner, not using a tabernacle, not a hut; but standing in a deep ditch; whence also some called him Gubba. And that name, if translated from the Syriac language into Greek, meaning 'λάκκον', that is, a lake. After that time, when the old man had escaped, he yielded to the beggars, and fixed a hut. Later, however, it was used to pray to family members, and also to small houses that were not their own, but those of others. And for twenty-five years he led a perpetual life in huts and cottages, so that the period of the struggle of seventy years is then summed up. But the food he used was not bread, nor vegetables, but purified barley, moistened only with water. But my mother, who was familiar to him, supplied this food for a very long time. But when on one occasion he came to her sick and learned that she would not be persuaded to take food suitable to the disease (for she too was now embracing monastic training), she advised him to yield to the physicians, and to consider that nourishment to be a medicine: for it is not used for pleasure, but for the sake of necessity. For I also, says he, who for forty years, as you know, have used barley alone, when a certain infirmity came upon me the day before this day, I ordered him who lived with me to ask for and bring me a little bread. For it occurred to me that if I died, I should give an account of my death before a just judge, as one who had shunned battles and despised the labors of servitude. For with a little food death could be prevented, and I could remain thus in this life, toiling and distressing myself, and gathering the riches which are perceived from these, I thought it more desirable to die of hunger than to live. Filled with fear, therefore, when I wanted to cut off the thorns of thought, I ordered to ask for bread, and ate what was brought; and I command you to give me no more barley, but to provide me with bread. From that tongue, therefore, we have heard, from every falsehood, that he ate barley for forty years. And these facts are indeed sufficient to guess how active and how laborious the man was in his monastic training.

But we will declare integrity and simplicity of behavior by other means. For after Flavianus had been ordained to feed the great flock of God and had learned the virtue of a man (for he was preached and was on everyone's lips), he actually took him down from the top of the mountain, as if the accusation had been brought to him. But since the proposed sacrifice was a mystical one, he brings it to the altar and recruits him into the number of priests. Now after the sacred office was finished, and this was made known to him by someone (for he was entirely ignorant of what had been done), he at first proceeded with all curses and abuses; but afterwards, taking a staff (for he was wont to enter leaning on it because of the old man), he himself pursued the priest, and as many others as were present. For he believed that the organization was his privacy and the top of the mountain, and that which he longed for in his way of life. But then some of his family members hardly calmed his anger. Now after the circle of the week was ended, and the day of the feast of Sunday came again, Flavianus the great again approached him, asking him to be a partaker of this celebration with them; But he said to those who had come: The things that have been done for you are not enough; but do you want to make me a priest again? But when they said that it was impossible for the same arrangement to take place twice, he did not yield, nor did he come, until time and his relatives taught him this. I know, indeed, that when this has been narrated, it will seem to many not to be so surprising; but I have put it down, so that those who think it worthy of commemoration may be sufficiently inferred from it, and the simplicity of his mind and the purity of his soul. But to those who are of this kind, the Lord has promised the kingdom of heaven: For, he says, "Amen, I say to you, unless you are converted like these little girls, you will not enter the kingdom of heaven" (Matt. 18). Since then, we have shown in summary the form and character of his soul, let us also show his trust in virtue.

 A certain captain of soldiers, who delighted in hunting, went up into the mountain to hunt. And dogs and soldiers followed him, and whatever was fit for hunting. But after he had seen a man at a distance, and had heard from those who were with him who he was, he immediately dismounted from his horse, approached, and spoke to him, and asked what he was doing and staying here; But he, on the other hand, asked in turn: But what did you come here to do? And when the leader had said: He will hunt: And I, he said, I am hunting my God, and I desire to catch him, and I long to behold him; nor will I cease from this beautiful hunt. When the captain heard this, and was equally surprised, he retired.

 Now when the city, incited by some evil demon, was roused to death, and the statues of the emperor were enraged, some of the most distinguished leaders came, who brought against the city a sentence of extermination. And when he had come down from the mountain, he detained the two approaching leaders in the marketplace. But when they had learned who he was, they jumped down from their horses, took hold of their hands and knees, and signaled their greetings to him. And he commanded that they should tell the emperor that he was a man, and that he had the same nature as those who had insulted him; and when anger must be measured by nature, let anger be used immoderately, and instead of its images it kills the images of God, and instead of bronze statues, it delivers bodies to death; and indeed for us it is readily available and easy to mold bronzes and to mold them again. but you, even if you are an emperor, cannot bring slain bodies back to life. And what do I mean by bodies? for you cannot reproduce a single hair. He said this in a Syriac voice. But they, hearing the interpreter translate into the Greek language, were terrified, and signified that they would pass it on to the emperor. But I think that all will confess that these words are the grace of the divine Spirit. For how else could he have spoken these things, a man truly learned in all things, but brought up in the fields, and living his life on the summits of the mountains, yet all round in simplicity, and who had not even spared himself divine speeches? When, therefore, I have explained his spiritual wisdom, and the confidence which belongs to the just (for the just trusts like a lion (Prov. 28), I will pass on to miracles.

 A certain wife of a wealthy nobleman had fallen ill with the disease of the scrotum; and some indeed called it a disease, the operation or vexation of a demon, while others thought it a weakness of the body. But whether it was this or that, it was of this kind. They said that if she ate thirty chickens a day, she could not quench her appetite with satiety, but still craved other things. When then, her resources were thus spent in her, those who were concerned with her should beg that divine man to have mercy on her. And he indeed came and prayed: and when he had placed the right hand of water, and had formed a sign of salutation, and commanded him to drink, he cured the disease, and so moderated that immoderate appetite, that thenceforth some small piece of fowl fulfilled the habit of feeding him daily. Indeed, this disease was treated in this way.

 But when a certain girl was still confined in a room and had suddenly begun to be tormented by an evil demon, the father ran to the divine man, praying and shouting, and demanding that his daughter be taken care of. And when he had prayed, he ordered the demon to depart from the girl at once. But he said that he had not entered it of his own free will but had been compelled by magical tricks. He also said that the name of the one who forced him, and the custom, were the cause of the enchantment. But when he had said these things, the father did not take a fit of anger, nor did he wait for the girl to be taken care of; but he goes to the highest of all magistrates, that is to say the governor who was in charge of several nations, accuses the man, and tells the matter. But the accused, being brought to trial, denied the matter, and called the accusation slander. Now he cited no other witness than the demon himself who had been the minister of incantation: and he begged the judge to run to that divine man and take his testimony. But when he said that it was neither fair nor just that the question should be held in the place of monastic training, the girl's father said that he would bring the Macedonian to trial; and running persuaded and led. But the judge, sitting outside the court, was not a judge, but a spectator. For Macedonius the Great performed the office of judge, using the power which dwelt within him. And when he commanded the demon to tell the usual lie, and to tell the tragedy with all the truth of the matter, he was driven by the greatest necessity, and showed the man who had brought him strength by magic charms, and the maid by whom that potion had been given to the girl. But when another was about to say what he had done under the compulsion of others, burning the house of one, killing the cattle of another, and inflicting some other damage on another, the man of God commanded him to be silent, and at once to withdraw far from the girl and from the city. But he, as one obeying the Lord's law, did as he was commanded, and immediately fled. Thus, when the divine man had delivered this man from wrath, he also delivered that wretch from the accusation, and prevented the judge from passing upon him the sentence of the capital, saying that it was not right that capital punishment should be decreed for those things which had been condemned by him, but rather that salvation should be given to him through repentance. And indeed, these things are sufficient to show the abundance of the divine power which had been given to him, yet I will tell others also.

A certain woman born in a noble place, and very rich (she was called Assyria) was indeed of an emotional mind, but she recognized no one of her household, but she could not bear to take food and drink. But most of the time he was constantly delirious, and this indeed others said was the harassment and operation of the devil; but the doctors said it was a disease of the brain. When, therefore, all the art had been exhausted, and no help could be given from it, her husband (he was Abrodianus), a man who was also one of the magistrates, and endowed with great dignity, running to that divine head, told the illness of the couple, and prayed that they might obtain a cure. . The divine man left, and indeed came home, and offered a prayer to God with great and intense zeal. And when he had finished his prayer, when he had ordered water to be brought, and had made the shape of a salutary seal, he ordered her to drink. But when the doctors stopped, because the disease had increased by drinking the cold water, the whole company was driven out, and he offered the woman a drink. And as soon as she had drunk it, she returned to herself, and being completely freed from the disease, she recognized the divine man, and begged him to take her right hand, and placed it on her eyes, and brought it to her mouth, and thereafter she was always in peace of mind.

But when that kind of life was embraced in the mountains, a certain shepherd, seeking the wandering sheep, came to that place where the man of God was (for it was a deep night, and much snow had fallen) and he saw, as he said, a pyre lighted around him, and some two-white clothed in clothing, they provided material for the fire. For by bringing cheerfulness to the soul, he enjoyed divine help.

Moreover, he was also a partaker of the prophetic gift. And when on one occasion there came to him a certain leader, famous for his piety and true religion (and who does not know the valor of Lupicianus?), he said that he was concerned about certain people who were bringing necessaries to him from the royal city by sea. For he said that fifty days had passed since they had left the port, but they had heard nothing of them. But he did not hesitate: One ship, my friend, has perished; and the other, the next day, will seize the port of Seleucia. And indeed, he heard that divine voice speak: but he learned by experience what he had said the truth.

But in order to pass over other things, I will relate those things which pertain to ourselves. When my mother had lived together with my father for thirteen years, she had not become the mother of children; for he was barren, so that anything bearing fruit was prevented by nature. And indeed, she did not bear it very painfully; for she who was learned in divine things believed that this was useful: but the father took great trouble that he should be deprived of his children, and, running round and round, begged the servants of God to ask him for children from God. Others, therefore, promised to supplicate themselves and to God, and commanded that he should be content with the will of God. Now this divine man openly professed that he would ask one thing from the workman of the universe, and he promised to accept the request. When three years had passed, and the promise had not been fulfilled, the father came again demanding the promise. And he commanded that his spouse should be sent to him. But when the mother had come, that divine man said that he would ask for her, and that she would receive his son, and that he should be dedicated to him who had given him. But when the mother only asked that she might receive the salvation of her soul, and that she might be delivered from hell: Besides this, she said, a generous and bountiful God will give you a son. For those who ask purely and sincerely, he grants double requests. From there the mother returned, bringing the promised blessing. And in the fourth year from this promise, she conceived, and bore in her womb; and he goes to the divine man, showing the hands of blessing. But in the fifth month from conception, there was a danger of miscarriage. And she again sent to her new wife Elisha (for sickness forbade him to come to him) and reminded him that she did not want to become the mother of children, and she brought him to the middle of his promises. But when he had seen him coming from a distance, he recognized him and indicated the cause; for the Lord had shown him both sickness and salvation at night. Then taking the staff, he came, leaning on it; and when he had been inside the house and had given the greeting of peace as he was accustomed to do. Be of good mind, he says, and do not be afraid; for the gift will not be taken away by him who gave it, unless you transgress the agreed agreements. But you are confident that you will return him to the one who has been given, and that you will consecrate him to the divine service. And so, said the mother, I both wish and will. For I consider that even the most imperfect fetus is more to be desired than the alien education of a child from God. When, therefore, he had received the water and had blessed it: Drink then, said the divine man, this water, and you will feel divine help. So, she drank as he was commanded, and escaped the danger of miscarriage. These are the miracles of our Elisha.

I often received his blessing and teaching. For, encouraging me, he often said: You were born, O son, with many labors; many nights I constantly asked God for this only, that your parents might become what they named you when you were born. See, then, that you live a life worthy of toil, that before you were born you were dedicated to the promises. But those things which are dedicated to God are to be venerated by all, and those which are not to be despised by the common people. It is fitting, then, that you also should not admit bad emotions; but do and think only those things which appease God, the lawgiver of virtue. The divine man continually advised me of these things; But I also remember what he said to me, and I was taught by a divine gift. But since I do not show my deeds what he urged me to do, I pray that through his prayers I may obtain divine help, and that the rest of my life I may do according to his precepts. What kind of person he was, and what labors he used to attract divine grace, these also are sufficient to teach.

But even in this world he received the honor worthy of his death for his labors. For all, both citizens and foreigners, and to whom the dispensation of the great magistrates had been entrusted, carrying that sacred bed on their shoulders, carried it into the house of the martyrs distinguished by victory; and together with the divine men Aphraates and Theodosius, they laid down that holy body and that which was acceptable to God: but the glory of such remained that it cannot be extinguished. But we, having put an end to the narrative, perceive him who can be perceived from the narrative as a good smell.

CHAPTER XIV. MAESYMAS

We know indeed that many other lights of piety and true religion shone in the city of Antioch, the great Severus, and Peter the Egyptian, Eutyches, and Cyril, and Moses, and Malchus, and many others also entered the same way. But if we were to try to write down the things that all have done in life, the whole time would not be enough for us: especially when the reading of too many would bring satiety. Therefore, of those who have been written, and of those who have been passed over, making conjectures about the lives of them, let them continue with praises and imitate them, and perceive benefit. But I will go over to the meadows of Cyrus and show the beauty of those who were in them, the fragrant and beautiful flowers, as much as I can.

There was a certain Maesymas, in those times which preceded us, a Syrian indeed by voice, and brought up in the country, and who showed every kind of virtue. But when he had become illustrious in that which is life in itself, he was entrusted with the care of a certain village. And when he sacrificed and fed God's sheep, he said and did what the divine law commanded. And they say that he did not often change his shirt or his shirt, but that by sewing some pieces of cloth to the tears which were made in them, he brought about a remedy in this way when he was old. And he cared for the guests and the poor with such zeal that he opened the doors to all who were present. For it is said that he had two barrels, one of corn, and the other of oil: from these he always supplied all those in need; and she was always full of the blessing which had been given to the widow of Sarephthana and had been cast into these vessels. For the Lord himself pours out all riches on all those who call upon him and like him he commanded the jar and the drop to spring forth, providing handfuls of the seeds of hospitality. So also, he presented to this admirable man a supply which corresponded equally to the enthusiasm of his spirit.

Now, indeed, he received great grace from the God of the universe to perform miracles as well. But I will make mention of one or two miracles; but I will pass over the rest, so that he may hasten to come to others.

A certain woman, adorned both in family and faith, offered her son, who had fallen ill (and he was at a very tender age), to many physicians. But the art being overcome, when the doctors had despaired, and had plainly declared that the child was going to die, the woman did not throw away a better hope, but imitated that of the Shunammites, and laid a chamber on the mule. And when he had placed himself and the child in it, he came to that divine man: and lamenting, and showing his affection for nature, he begged him to bring help. But when he had taken the child in his hands, and moved him to the base of the altar, he lay prostrate, begging a physician for souls and bodies; and having accepted the request, he returned the strong son to his mother. But I heard it from her who saw this miracle and received the salvation of the child.

And they say that when the master of that village also came (for this was Latoius, who indeed held the first parts of the Antiochian senate, but was held in the darkness of impiety) and exacted more fruit than was necessary from the farmers, that divine man consulted him for clemency, and spoke words of mercy to him and that he remained inexorable, but that he knew by experience the damage that followed from his failure to respond. For when it was necessary for him to go, and the carriage was ready, and he was sitting, he ordered the driver to spur the mules; indeed, they were pulling with all their strength, pressing and trying to carry away the shield: but the wheels were seen bound with iron and lead. But when a multitude of peasants, too, by moving the wheels with their bars, could do nothing, one of Latoius's friends, who sat by him, represented the cause to him, saying that the old priest had cursed him, and that he must be propitiated and rendered benevolent. Jumping therefore from the chariot, there was a suppliant to him whom he had previously rejected; and falling at his feet, and embracing the dirty cloths, begged him to control his anger. And when he had received the prayers, and had offered them to the Lord, he loosened the chains of the wheels which were not visible and caused the vehicle to ride as usual.

Moreover, they also tell many other things of this kind about that divine head. And it may be understood from these also, that to those who wish to philosophize, the delay which is dragged on in towns and villages brings no harm. For he shows here, and those who take care of God's culture like this, that even those who are engaged in the midst of the multitude of men can reach the very pinnacle of virtue.

Of which I hope to raise at least a small part, aided by their prayers.

CHAPTER XV: ACEPSIMAS

Acepsimas lived at this time, whose fame spread widely throughout the East (Theodor., book IV Hist., chap. 26). When he shut himself up in a little house, he passed sixty years, neither seeing nor speaking; but he turned to himself, and grasping God in his vision, there received all consolation, in accordance with the prophecy which says: Delight in the Lord, and pray to him, and he will give you the requests of your heart (Psal. 36). But extending his hand through a small ditch, he received what was brought for nourishment: but the ditch had not been dug in such a way as to tend at all in a straight line, lest it should be from the opposite side of those who wanted to see him, but it was oblique, and so constructed as to be like a curved line. Food was brought to him, and his lens was moistened with water: and once a week, going out at night, he drew from a nearby spring as much water as was sufficient. And when a certain shepherd, feeding his sheep at a distance, saw him moving in the dark, and guessed that he was a wolf, for he was walking stooped, as if he were heavily burdened with a sword, he moved his sling as if he were going to throw a stone. But when his hand remained motionless for a long time, and he could not throw the stone until that divine man returned after drinking water, he felt his ignorance, and after dawn he came to the gymnasium of virtue, and told what had happened, and asked for forgiveness, and received the remission of his offence; not heard by the speaking voice, but understood by the gestures of the hands as appeasement.

But someone else, being exercised by a certain malicious desire of inquiry, and desiring to know what he was continually doing all this time, ventured to climb the plane-tree, which was situated near the moat; but he at once perceived the fruits of his audacity. For the middle part of his body was dried up to his feet, and he was supple, accusing his sin. He, on the other hand, followed by the plantain tree, first signified future health. For lest another, when he had done similar things, should suffer similar punishments, he ordered the tree to be cut down; but the cutting of the tree was followed by the removal of the punishment. Indeed, this divine man used so much fortitude and forbearance: and he received so much grace from the Agonotes.

Now when he was preparing to emigrate, he foretold that after fifty days he would receive the end of his life: and he received all who wished to see him. And when the elders also came to the church, he indeed urged him to accept the yoke of the presbytery: I know, O father, the depth of your philosophy, and how great is my poverty; but since the administration of the priesthood has been entrusted to me, laying hands on it from this order and not from that order. Receive then, says he, the gift of the priesthood, ministering indeed with my right hand, and supplying the grace of the most holy Spirit. At this he is reported to have said that in a few days he will depart from here. for if I had lived longer, I would have completely avoided this heavy and terrible burden of the priesthood, fearing to give an account of what I had deposited. But since I was not so long ago going away, leaving those who are here, I do not seem reluctant to the orders. Immediately, then, without any guidance, he, indeed, bending his knees, awaited grace; but he, laying on his hand, was the administrator of the Spirit. But when, having received the priesthood, he had lived a few days, his life changed his life, and he accepted the elderly and experienced care, for this one was subject to much care.

But when they all wanted to snatch the body, and each had in mind to transfer it to his own village, one of them, having signified that he should swear by the saint, took up the contention. For he said that the saint had brought him under oath to deliver the burial in this place. Thus, even after death, the citizens of heaven took care of frugality and simplicity; and neither when they lived, did they ever bring into their minds that anything should make them great spirits, and the dead did not embrace the honor of men; but they transferred all their love to the bridegroom; not unlike chaste women, who seek to be loved and praised only by their spouses, despising the praises of others. For this reason, the bridegroom makes them famous and distinguished, even if they do not want it, and imparts glory to men from a kind of overflowing abundance. For when one who pursues the divine, asks for heavenly things, he also adds many other things along with them, giving multiplied requests. He also said this in giving the laws: Ask for the kingdom of God, and justice, and all other things will be added to you (Luke 12). And again: He who leaves father and mother, and brother and children for the sake of my gospel, will receive a hundredfold even in this world, and in the future will be the heir of eternal life. These things he said and did (Matt. 19).

It is for us, too, learned by word and work, and leaning on their prayers, as if to reach the goal, to reach the reward of the heavenly calling, which is in Christ Jesus our Lord.

CHAPTER XVI: MARON

I will remember Maron after this; for he also adorned the divine chorus of the saints. For having embraced life, which is made under God, he occupied a certain summit, which was held in honor by those who were once impious; and when he had consecrated to God what was in it the temple of the demons, he occupied himself in it, a small tabernacle fixed in it, which, however, he rarely used. And he not only used the usual labors, but also invented others, accumulating the wealth of philosophy; but the agonist measured his gratitude by his labors. For the liberal and munificent God gave him so abundantly the gift of healings, that his glory indeed spread to all parts, and he attracted all from every quarter, and experience taught him that his fame was true. For it was to be seen that fevers were extinguished with the dew of blessing, and horrors ceased, and demons fled, and various diseases of every kind were cured with one medicine. For the physicians present to each disease the appropriate medicine, but the supplication of the saints is the common remedy for all diseases.

And he not only cured the ailments of the body, but also offered appropriate treatment to the soul; taking care of the covetousness of the latter, and the wrath of the latter; and presenting to one the doctrine of moderation, to the other the discipline of justice, and indeed chastising the intemperance of the latter, and exciting the dullness of the latter. Using this for agriculture, he made many plants of philosophy; and the garden which now sprouts in the region of Cyrus, he himself planted for God. The work of this planting is the great James, to whom he drew that prophetic voice: "Like the cedar that is in Lebanon, it shall multiply" (Ps. 101); and also, all the others, of which, if God wills, I will mention them separately.

And thus, bearing the divine care of agriculture, and taking care of souls and bodies at the same time, he suffered a little illness, that we might learn both the weakness of nature and the strength of the mind, he indeed departed from life.

But a bitter war broke out between the neighbors. And from the neighbors a certain village, the most crowded with people, when he had arrived with all the people forced at once, he indeed smote others and put them to flight; and having built a great house, they enjoy the benefit of it to this day, honoring that distinguished conqueror with a public and celebrated festival.

But even we who are absent enjoy the blessing, for our memory suffices as a reminder.

CHAPTER XVIII: EUSEBIUS

I will also add to the aforementioned saints the great Eusebius, who died not long ago (Theodor., book IV Hist., chapter 26). And when he had lived for many years, he indeed endured labor equal to time, and at the same time he chose courage equal to labor. And he brought back a manifold profit from it; for in the greatness of the rewards the athlete surpasses the competition. Here, then, when he had first believed the care of others for his faith, he was led by what they led; for they too were men of divine virtue and athletes and exercisers; and when he had spent some time with them, and had received a good and correct knowledge of philosophy, he embraced the monastic life; and when he had occupied a certain ridge of the mountain (and the largest village, which they call Asichus, is close to him), a ditch was made only, and the stones were not even joined with mud, he passed the rest of his life under the god, afflicting himself, indeed covered with skins; but chickpeas and beans moistened with water nourished themselves. Quinete sometimes also fed on carrion, thus trying in any way to support the infirmity of his body. And when he had reached the extreme of old age, so that he had also lost most of his teeth, he neither changed his food nor his dwelling. But even when he was frozen in winter and burned in summer, he strongly bore the opposite qualities of the air, having indeed a wrinkled face, but all the limbs of his body were parched. And his body was consumed by so many labors, that the girdle did not even remain above the loins but fell below; for there was nothing to forbid it; for both the buttocks and hips were consumed, and the girdle afforded an easy descent to the lower ones. So, he put on the girdle of his coat, devising to stand on this account.

But it was difficult for him to converse with many people. For when he constantly grasped the divine contemplation by vision, he did not want to withdraw his mind from it; but still, although he was endowed with such intense love, he allowed some of his acquaintances to remove that which blocked the gate, and to enter; and when he had expounded to them the doctrine from the divine discourses, he again ordered them to put mud on the gates as they departed. But when he thought it altogether better to avoid an encounter even with a few, he completely barred the approach by throwing a great stone at the gate. And through a ditch he was talking with a few of his relatives, but he was not seen. For thus he had provided. And from there it also received a little nourishment. But again, he had refused to speak with everyone, he only deigned to speak to me with that sweet and God-pleasing voice, and he often detained me when I wanted to go away, discussing heavenly things. But when many came to him and asked for the good of a blessing, and the tumult bore him with difficulty, neither considering his old age, nor deeming his infirmity urgent, he crossed a moat which could not easily be crossed even by the strong and willing. and when he had come to a certain nearby fleet of monks, a small ditch was again brought to the corner of the wall, and he struggled with his usual labors.

And the commander of this flock, a man full of all virtue, said that when he had eaten fifteen caricas, he had passed seven weeks of holy fasting. And this struggle he underwent, when he had lived more than ninety years, and he was afflicted with a weakness which cannot be told: but the weakness was overcome by the zeal of the soul, and the love of God made all things easy and expedient. When he was covered with such sweat, he reached the finish line of the race, and seeing the athlete, and longing for the crown.

But I pray that I may obtain that intercession, which I have hitherto received while I was still alive. For I believe that he lives and has a purer trust in God.

CHAPTER XIX: SALAMANUS

Thinking that I should do an injustice to virtue, if I did not mention the admirable life of Salamanus to posterity, but neglected to be overwhelmed by oblivion, I would summarize the narrative. There is a certain village to the west of the river Euphrates, overlooking the bank itself, and it is called Capersana. When he rose from it, when he had embraced a quiet life, and had found a little house in the street opposite, he shut himself up in it, leaving neither door nor window. But once a year digging the ground, he received the nourishment of the whole year, never speaking to any man. And he continued to do this, not for a short time, but for a very long time. Moreover, the priest of the city of which that village was, when he had learned the man's prowess, came, desiring to give him the gift of the priesthood; and the little house having been pierced in some part, he entered; and he laid his hand, and performed the prayer, and indeed said to him many times, and that which had come to him signified the grace. But when he heard no voice, he went away, ordering that the moat be built again. On another occasion, however, those who were of the village from which he had set out, when they had crossed the river by night, and having penetrated the house, receiving him neither resisting nor commanding, expelled him into their own village; and when they had built such a little house towards the East, they immediately enclosed it. And he was likewise quiet while speaking with him. But after a few days, those who were in that village, which is from the opposite side, when they had attacked again by night, and having penetrated the house, they abducted him to them, neither resisting, nor to remain urgent, nor retreating again in a prompt and eager spirit. Thus, he established himself as completely dead to the world, and speaking truly with that apostolic voice, he said: I have been crucified with Christ. But I live, it is no longer I, but Christ lives in me. Now that I live in Christ, I live in the faith of the Son of God, who loved me and gave himself for me (Gal. 2). Such was the case here too. For these things are sufficient to show the whole plan of his life.

But when I receive a blessing from him also, I will pass to another.

CHAPTER XX: MARIS

There is a certain village in Homer which we call Netis. When the god of the sea had built with him a small house, he remained shut up in it for thirty-seven years. But from a mountain situated near it, it received a great deal of moisture. And in the season of winter also certain drops of water emanated into it. But how much damage arises from this to bodies, both citizens and countrymen know; for even those who live in the fields, the diseases that arise from it are manifest. But even these things did not persuade that holy head to change his house; but he continued strongly and steadily until he had finished the course.

Moreover, he also spent his previous life with the labors of virtue: whence he preserved chastity both in body and soul; and this he himself plainly signified to me, teaching that his body had remained whole and uncorrupted, and in the state in which he had come out of his mother's womb, and that when he had indeed celebrated the feasts of the martyrs on many days when he was a youth, and had charmed the people with the goodness of his voice. For most of the time he continued to dance and was remarkable for the beauty of his body. But still, neither the appearance of the body, nor the clarity of the voice, nor the meeting that intervened with many people, brought any harm to the beauty of the soul; But he also increased his strength by the labors which he endured in confinement.

I have often used this custom; for he ordered the door to be opened for me; He embraced me as I came, and on philosophy, he made use of a rambling and long-winded speech.

Moreover, here too he was remarkable for his simplicity, and he absolutely abhorred various manners. But he loved poverty more than abundance. At ninety years of age, he used to wear clothes woven from goat hair. But bread and a little salt fulfilled his use of nourishment. But since he longed for a long time to see a spiritual and mystical sacrifice offered, he asked that an offering of the divine gift be made there. I, however, willingly agreed; and I ordered the sacred vessels to be brought (for the village was not far off), and for the use of the altar, in the hands of the deacons, I offered a mystical, divine, and salutary sacrifice. But he was filled with all spiritual pleasure, and thought that he himself saw heaven, and said that he had never received such joy.

But as I was greatly beloved by him, I thought that I would be doing him wrong if I did not also praise the dead, and if I did not propose to others this excellent philosophy for them to imitate. Now therefore, as I pray to obtain his help, I will put an end to the narrative.

The Scriptorium Project is the work of a small group of lay people of various apostolic churches who are interested in the preservation, transmission, and translation of the works of the early and medieval church. Our efforts are to make the works of the church fathers accessible to anyone who might have an interest in Christian antiquities and the theological, philosophical, and moral writings that have become the bedrock of Western Civilization.

To-date, our releases have pulled from the Greek, Syriac, Georgian, Latin, Celtic, Ethiopian, and Coptic traditions of Christianity, and have been pulled from sundry local traditions and languages.

PHILOTHEUS OR THEOPHILOS

www.ingramcontent.com/pod-product-compliance
Lightning Source LLC
LaVergne TN
LVHW052049070526
838201LV00086B/5140